HAWAII
R E E F
Fish

ISLAND HERITAGE
Honolulu, Hawai'i

Contents

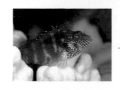

Acknowledgments

We would like to thank the following persons who assisted and contributed to this publication:

John E. Randall, a diving pioneer and head of ichthyology at the Bishop Museum, who made tropical marine fish identification, as we know it today, possible. He was kind enough to assist with the identification of some of the species in this book, as well as many other species we encountered and photographed in other areas of the Pacific.

Our diving and traveling friends who share our interest and enthusiasm to observe, identify and photograph marine life.

Fair Wind and *Sea Paradise* (Keauhou Bay), who allowed us to utilize their vessels to take photographs.

Live/Dive Pacific, whose vessels, the Kona Aggressor I & II, provided the perfect platform for ourselves, along with other contributing photographers, to learn and pursue underwater photography in Hawaii.

Susan Davis, who made our first three books possible and who has always shared her time and printing expertise with us as well as becoming a wonderful friend.

Keoki Stender who edited the text, and contributed his scientific knowledge, suggestions and photographs and was a pleasure to work with.

Photo Credits:
Keoki Stender: Flying Gurnard, Pearl Wrasse,
    Viper Moray
Mike and Pauline Severns:
    Masked Angelfish (male and female),
    Yellow Anthias
Steven Carothers: Bullethead Parrotfish
Jamie Dickey: Titan Scorpionfish
Glen Fowler: Speckled Scorpionfish
Ray Mock: Barred Moray and Rockmover.
Gui Garcia: Spotted Seahorse

All other photographs, including cover, by authors
Astrid Witte and Casey Mahaney
© Blue Kirio, utilizing Nikon 8008S cameras in Ikelite
underwater housings.

**A sincere "Mahalo Nui Loa" to Fuji Film who
provided us with Velvia and Provia Chrome
Film for this project.**

Introduction

When entering the underwater world, most divers and snorkelers are first captivated by the dazzling array of tropical fish. Showing off their colors with darting and swirling motions, these living gems cause the reef to explode with life.

Exploring the coral reef is one of the most rewarding quests to Mother Nature's realm one may experience. Contrary to visiting the forest or other terrestrial wildlife environments, close-up encounters with spectacular wildlife are common on the reef. Many of the fish are easily and safely observed even by first time snorkelers.

Intrigued with the beauty of the marine environment, most people soon begin to inquire about the many different fish they see, and perhaps learn that many of the most colorful fish are butterflyfishes, and the Hawaiian name for Hawaii's State fish is Humuhumu nukunuku apua'a. Although fascinated, few divers or snorkelers learn more than just a handful of names. While on vacation, few people have the desire to seriously study and digest difficult-to-comprehend scientific information.

Since awareness of the reef inhabitants' natural environment and behavior and knowing the species' name will lead to an even greater, much more rewarding experience, we've designed this book to accommodate the layperson's need for an organized, easy-to-use identification guide. If you can remember just a few basic trademarks about the fish, you're likely to quickly locate it in this guide.

HOW TO USE THIS BOOK

We have organized the fish families by their trademarks which are most obvious to the layperson. In order to quickly locate the observed fish in this guide and identify it, it is helpful to acquire at least a very basic knowledge of terms and to note obvious markings, shape, size or behavior, while observing the fish. Try to remember if the fish you noticed was lying motionless on the bottom (on sand? On rocks? On coral?), or was it darting in and out of coral? Or perhaps it hovered several feet above the reef?

If it was swimming, was it primarily using its dorsal (top) fin or the pectoral (side) fins? If you prefer, carry an underwater slate with you, to jot down this basic information. Once back on the boat or the beach, compare your notes with the trademarks in the guide.

For example:

TRADEMARKS	FAMILIES
Large discs and ovals	Butterflyfishes, Surgeonfishes (Tangs)
Swims with pectoral fins	Wrasses, Parrotfishes
Small bottom dwellers	Blennies, Gobies

Once you learn how to differentiate the various fish families, it will become even easier to quickly identify each species.

INFORMATION PROVIDED

COMMON NAMES provide snorkelers and divers with a way of communicating in simple English. However, since common names may vary in different regions and countries, we have included the **SCIENTIFIC NAMES** to cross reference with other marine life identification books. The **HAWAIIAN NAME** is included if available. The **AVERAGE SIZE** mentioned is at maturity of the species. The **DIET** consists of food the particular species normally feeds on. Marine life (like other wildlife) spend their time either resting or actively feeding and/or pursuing prey. Being aware of its food source can assist you with finding the animal. Fish that feed on zooplankton, for instance, are most likely to be spotted above and off the reef, rather than tucked away in the coral. However, animals often "adjust their diet" when humans interact (see fish feeding). **DESCRIPTION AND DISTINCTIVE FEATURES** will help fish watchers with detailed identification information, especially when identifying from a photograph.

Besides the anatomical changes, color patterns and marking are what distinguish one fish species from another. See page 8 for the most commonly used terms to describe anatomical features, colors and markings in layman's terms. Keep in mind that many fish species display a variety of color patterns, with some changing gradually with age or sex, while others change color patterns in a flash for camouflage, courting or mating rituals, or while feeding.

We also provide you with information on **Where to find them**. This section describes the most likely environment and depth range. This category also states if the species only exists in Hawaii. Most species that are not endemic to Hawaii exist throughout the Tropical Pacific, with some species' distribution extending into the Indian Ocean, and a few being circumtropical. Observations on behavioral traits are personal observations of the authors as well as recorded scientific information.

Venomous fish species are marked with a "V".

LIKE NOWHERE ELSE

The Hawaiian Islands are the most isolated islands in the world. Over 2000 miles of deep ocean separate them from the nearest continental land mass. Since marine life dispersal takes place during the larval stage, when the plants and animals are small and buoyant, Hawaiian marine life depended on ocean currents to migrate to the archipelago. How long they can float is determined by the species' duration of larval life. The strength and direction of the ocean currents determine how far the organism can be carried during this time. Unfortunately, the prevailing currents don't favor Hawaii to the degree they support other parts of the Pacific. As a result, less species were able to reach and settle in Hawaiian waters. The Hawaiian native marine life has benefited from a unique evolution over time, resulting in a number of species which are endemic to Hawaii. About 30% of Hawaii's fishes are found nowhere else in the world. To emphasize this unique phenomenon we have marked the

DISTINCTIVE FEATURES

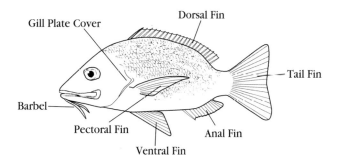

Gill Plate Cover
Dorsal Fin
Tail Fin
Barbel
Pectoral Fin
Anal Fin
Ventral Fin

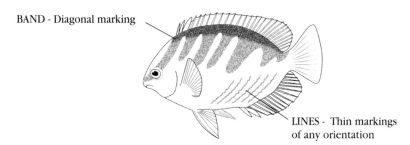

BAND - Diagonal marking

LINES - Thin markings of any orientation

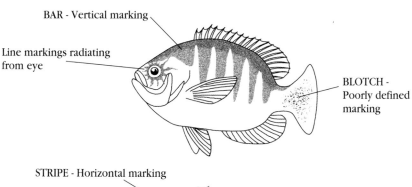

BAR - Vertical marking

Line markings radiating from eye

BLOTCH - Poorly defined marking

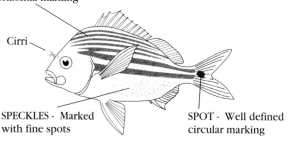

STRIPE - Horizontal marking

Cirri

SPECKLES - Marked with fine spots

SPOT - Well defined circular marking

endemic species "E".

SYMBIOTIC RELATIONSHIPS

Symbiosis is a relationship in which two organisms live in intimate association, and at least one of them benefits. Many marine animals depend on symbiotic relationships for food, transportation or other benefits necessary for survival.

Mutualism is a form of symbiotic relationships, where both organisms benefit. The Hawaiian Cleaner Wrasse and its host are the classic example. The host benefits because parasites, diseased tissue and excess mucus are removed. The wrasse benefits since the host's parasites provide food. The wrasse represents neither prey nor predator to other organisms, and its approach is readily welcomed by the host. The cleaners can be observed entering the frightening mouth of a moray to deliver a complete cleaning service. Although the moray could have an easy meal, it would never attempt to eat the cleaner.

Another representative for mutualism is the Hawaiian Shrimp Goby, which shares a burrow with a blind shrimp. The shrimp builds and maintains the burrow, while the goby, with superior eyesight warns the shrimp when a potential predator approaches.

Commensalism is formed when two symbionts enter an intimate association in which neither one will harm the other, but one may benefit from the other.

The Blue Goatfish often follows the Rockmover, Wrasse when feeding. The Rockmover, which turns over rocks in search of prey, does not get harmed by the goatfish, but the goatfish benefits by feeding on the leftovers of the Rockmover.

A symbiotic relationship is considered **parasitic** if one symbiont, the parasite, takes advantage of its host, such as feeding on the host's eggs or even on the host itself.

UNDERWATER PHOTOGRAPHY

Before you become involved with underwater photography, you should master your diving or snorkeling skills and feel very comfortable in the water. Shallow water (no deeper than 10 feet) snapshots of reef scenes can be accomplished with waterproof disposable cameras, which are available virtually everywhere. When attempting to shoot portraits of marine animals, it is necessary to go a step further and acquire a more "serious" (i.e. expensive) system. Since color is lost at depth, you need to use an underwater strobe for your photography in order to get good results. The Nikonos and Sea & Sea cameras are two choices which can be combined with a strobe. Both utilize a framer system for close-up photography. Since the Nikonos provides superior results, we'll refer in this publication to the Nikonos framer setup, but similar images can be produced with the Sea & Sea cameras. The Nikonos can also be used with either the "close up kit" which is ideal for subjects sized at about 8 inches, or the "macro kit", which is used for subjects ranging between 1/2 inch and 2 inches. The disadvantage of both the Nikonos and the Sea & Sea is that the subject needs to be placed inside the framer in order to produce a focused image. Unfortunately, few fish are willing "to jump through the hoop."

For those "difficult" cases it becomes necessary to use a SLR camera (autofocus or manual focus) and place it in a specially designed underwater housing. This system has endless possibilities, but is more expensive. (See references for recommended books with more detailed information.)

A NOTE ON FEEDING FISHES

We, as snorkelers and divers, should remember that Mother Ocean's "pets" don't always play by human rules. It's their world we are invading. Let's not blame them for our ignorance. Most fish, small or large, are naturally shy and flee upon a diver's approach. Once accustomed to human interaction and feeding sessions, some of them quickly overcome any shyness and not only "bully" more timid species off the reef, but also become extremely competitive and aggressive when engaging in these unnatural feeding frenzies. This abnormal behavior is often redirected toward humans (accidentally), in their attempt to get their share of the free meal. Fingers can easily be mistaken for food and get bitten, which in the case of a butterflyfish is not too serious, but an eel can cause major damage. Fish in the Surgeonfish (Tang) family possess razor-like scalpels that have been known to seriously slice (19 stitches) a snorkeler feeding a group of fish. The fish just got excited and in the frenzy sliced the feeder. Be aware that eels and other predators hunt mostly by smell. So even if you are not currently engaging in the feeding, but recently touched fish food, such as squid for instance, they may very well mistake your hand for food.

Again, most fish species, including eels and sharks, are naturally quite timid. If you don't feed them, they won't feed on you! So remember, if you must feed the fish, don't blame them if they bite or injure you.

Large Ovals and Discs

Butterflyfishes – Moorish Idols – Surgeonfishes

Large Ovals and Discs

Butterflyfishes – Moorish Idols – Surgeonfishes

Family: Butterflyfishes - *Chaetodontidae*

Some of the most eye-catching fishes are in the butterflyfish family. Though the species vary greatly in their striking patterns and colorations, butterflyfishes share some common features. They feed during daylight hours. Their diet ranges from plankton to small invertebrates, depending on the species. Generally they are home-ranging and many are thought to pair for life. During the night, butterflyfishes "sleep" in a crevice or coral head. It is during this time that divers or snorkelers can observe them in their more somber color stage. If exposed to artificial light (flashlight), they will soon return to their daytime color pattern. Their reproduction process usually occurs at dusk, with the simultaneous release and fertilization of eggs into the current. After hatching, juveniles seek the protection of shallow bays, while mature butterflyfishes usually prefer seaward reefs.

Photography: Most butterflyfishes feature spectacular color patterns and are quite easily approached and therefore are some of the most desirable subjects for underwater photographers. For a daytime portrait shot, 60mm and 105mm macro lenses are a good choice, while stunning wide angle shots of paired or schooling butterflyfishes are possible with lenses ranging from 35mm - 15mm. At night, when the butterflyfishes are in their dormant state, it is sometimes possible to place a Nikonos 28mm or 35mm close-up framer around the fish.

COMMON NAME: Tinker's Butterflyfish

SCIENTIFIC NAME: *Chaetodon tinkeri*

AVERAGE SIZE: 5-6 inches
DESCRIPTION AND DISTINCTIVE FEATURES: Black spots on white body, golden bar through eye, golden markings on dorsal fin, base of pectoral fins, and snout, golden tail.
DIET: Varied, mostly planktonic invertebrates.
WHERE TO FIND THEM: Due to over-collecting, this naturally uncommon fish is now rare in depths above the recreational dive limit. At less-dived sites, they can occasionally be observed at depths as shallow as 60 feet. This species was believed to be endemic, but has recently been observed at scattered Micronesian locations.
OBSERVATIONS: Once encountered, this stunning butterflyfish is easily approached, which unfortunately may have contributed to its over-collection.

COMMON NAME: Reticulated Butterflyfish

SCIENTIFIC NAME: *Chaetodon reticulatus*

AVERAGE SIZE: 5 - 6 inches
DESCRIPTION AND DISTINCTIVE FEATURES: A spectacular body color pattern based on whitish-yellow and black. Red marking on anal fin. Yellow eye-band, yellow band on anal fin and tail.
DIET: Coral polyps, algae.
WHERE TO FIND THEM: An uncommon species found on coral reefs at depths ranging from 10 feet to 90 feet.
OBSERVATIONS: Relatively shy upon divers' approach. Patient, unobtrusive divers can often get quite close. Mostly seen in pairs.

COMMON NAME: Blacklip or Klein's Butterflyfish

SCIENTIFIC NAME: *Chaetodon kleinii*
HAWAIIAN NAME: Lauhau
AVERAGE SIZE: 4 inches
DESCRIPTION AND DISTINCTIVE FEATURES:
Dirty-yellowish body. Dark bar through
eye which has bluish sheen at top, dark
lips.

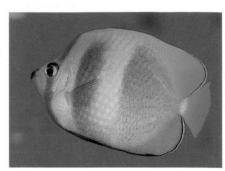

DIET: Zooplankton.
WHERE TO FIND THEM: Quite common on
the reef, or feeding above the reef in the
water column at a depth below 60 feet.
OBSERVATIONS: Approachable by the unobtrusive diver.

COMMON NAME: Speckled or Citrus Butterflyfish

SCIENTIFIC NAME: *Chaetodon citrinellus*
HAWAIIAN NAME: Lauhau
AVERAGE SIZE: 3 - 5 inches
**DESCRIPTION AND DISTINCTIVE
FEATURES:** Broad black bar
through eye. Often confused
with milletseed butterflyfish, but
note that this species has no
black spot on base of tail, but
black markings on the anal fin
and its body is pale yellow

rather than bright yellow. The dark spots are arranged into diagonal rows.
DIET: Algae, coral polyps, small invertebrates.
WHERE TO FIND THEM: Prefers shallow reefs. Rare in Hawaii.
OBSERVATIONS: Generally seen in pairs. Can be quite skittish.

COMMON NAME: Lemon or Milletseed Butterflyfish   E

SCIENTIFIC NAME: *Chaetodon miliaris*
HAWAIIAN NAME: Lau wiliwili
AVERAGE SIZE: 4 inches
DESCRIPTION AND DISTINCTIVE FEATURES:
Dark eye-bar, bright yellow body with ver-
tically arranged speckles and large black
spot a base of tail.

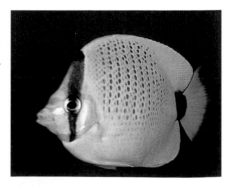

DIET: Zooplankton, fish eggs.
WHERE TO FIND THEM: Most commonly
observed feeding in the water column
above the reef in depths ranging from 6
feet to beyond the recreational dive limit.

A common species that is only found in Hawaii.

OBSERVATIONS: This species is not just common, it is also very bold. Most often it is seen in large schools feeding in the water column, but these schools can be observed indulging on the Sergeant Major's eggs. This butterflyfish is also common in snorkeling spots, where they take advantage of handouts. No matter if you encounter this species in its natural state or an area where fish feeding is practiced, this butterflyfish is easily approached.

COMMON NAME: Pebbled or Multiband Butterflyfish   E

SCIENTIFIC NAME: *Chaetodon multicinctus*

HAWAIIAN NAME: Kikākapu
AVERAGE SIZE: 4 inches
DESCRIPTION AND DISTINCTIVE FEATURES: Black eye-bar, small black band at base of tail and edge of tail and five beige vertical bands on its cream colored body. These bands appear at times only faintly.
DIET: Coral polyps.
WHERE TO FIND THEM: On the reef in depths ranging from 10 feet to 90 feet. Endemic to Hawaii.

OBSERVATIONS: Seen in pairs or small groups. This species is more timid than the Lemon Butterflyfish, but can be approached by the controlled diver.

COMMON NAME: Saddleback Butterflyfish

SCIENTIFIC NAME: *Chaetodon ephippium*

HAWAIIAN NAME: Kikākapu
AVERAGE SIZE: 7 - 9 inches
DESCRIPTION AND DISTINCTIVE FEATURES: This species is easily recognized by its spectacular color patterns: Golden snout and chest, larger black patch on upper part of body, including dorsal fin, white line around black patch. Also note red marking at base of tail and blue stripes along sides of body.
DIET: Coral polyps, sponges, small invertebrates, fish eggs, algae.
WHERE TO FIND THEM: Relatively uncommon in Hawaii. May be observed in a variety of habitats at depths of 10-90 feet.
OBSERVATIONS: Generally occurs in pairs. Usually skittish towards approaching divers.

COMMON NAME: Threadfin Butterflyfish

SCIENTIFIC NAME: *Chaetodon auriga*

HAWAIIAN NAME: Kikākapu
AVERAGE SIZE: 6 - 8 inches
DESCRIPTION AND DISTINCTIVE FEATURES: Two sets of diagonal lines on white body, turning gold in back, black bar through eye, black spot on dorsal fin. One elongated dorsal ray.
DIET: Coral polyps, algae, worms.
WHERE TO FIND THEM: Common on reefs in depths ranging from below 6 to 50 feet.
OBSERVATIONS: Mostly seen in pairs, staying close to their home territory. Threadfin Butterflyfish sometimes react skittish toward divers and are difficult to get close to.

COMMON NAME: Lined Butterflyfish

SCIENTIFIC NAME: *Chaetodon lineolatus*

HAWAIIAN NAME: Kikākapu
AVERAGE SIZE: 10 - 12 inches
DESCRIPTION AND DISTINCTIVE FEATURES: The largest of all the butterflyfishes found in Hawaii. Similar to Threadfin Butterflyfish, but has only one set of black vertical lines on body and has broad black marking below dorsal fin/base of tail, which the threadfin does not have.
DIET: Coral polyps, small invertebrates and algae.
WHERE TO FIND THEM: On shallow reefs, but has been reported at great depths. Uncommon in Hawaii.
OBSERVATIONS: Almost always observed in pairs and usually skittish and difficult to approach. The exception being in areas where fish feeding is practiced. Here, they overcome their natural shyness and approach divers and snorkelers boldly.

COMMON NAME: Bluestripe Butterflyfish   E

SCIENTIFIC NAME: *Chaetodon fremblii*

HAWAIIAN NAME: Kikākapu
AVERAGE SIZE: 4 - 5 inches
DESCRIPTION AND DISTINCTIVE FEATURES:
Bright blue stripes on yellow body, black spot on forehead, large black and smaller white spot at base of tail.
DIET: Small invertebrates and algae.
WHERE TO FIND THEM: This endemic species is relatively common in shallow areas, but has also been reported from great depths.
OBSERVATIONS: Quite approachable by an unobtrusive diver.

COMMON NAME: Ornate Butterflyfish

SCIENTIFIC NAME: *Chaetodon ornatissimus*
HAWAIIAN NAME: Kikākapu
AVERAGE SIZE: 6 - 8 inches
DESCRIPTION AND DISTINCTIVE FEATURES:
Six flamboyant orange diagonal bands on side of body, yellow and black markings on face, edges of all fins and tail.
DIET: Feeds exclusively on live coral polyps.
WHERE TO FIND THEM: On rich coral reefs in depths ranging from 10 to 90 feet. As juveniles, they can be seen singularly within the protection of coral branches.

OBSERVATIONS: Adults are home-ranging and always seen in pairs. In spite of its color pattern, this species is not collected for aquaria, due to its feeding habits. This may contribute to its relatively common occurrence.

COMMON NAME: Oval or Redfin Butterflyfish

SCIENTIFIC NAME: *Chaetodon lunulatus*

HAWAIIAN NAME: Kapuhili
AVERAGE SIZE: 4 - 5 inches
DESCRIPTION AND DISTINCTIVE FEATURES:
Vertical black eye bar, bluish stripes on body, distinctive red anal fin.
DIET: Coral polyps.
WHERE TO FIND THEM: In shallow coral-rich areas down to depths of 60 feet.
OBSERVATIONS: An uncommon species that almost exclusively occurs in pairs. Their reaction to divers ranges from skittish to quite approachable.

COMMON NAME: Racoon Butterflyfish

SCIENTIFIC NAME: *Chaetodon lunula*

HAWAIIAN NAME: Kikākapu
AVERAGE SIZE: 6 - 7 inches
DESCRIPTION AND DISTINCTIVE FEATURES: Broad black bar over eye, bordered by white bar. Broad black bar on body. Note overall dusky-yellow color and black spot at base of tail.
DIET: Small invertebrates, fish eggs, coral polyps and algae.
WHERE TO FIND THEM: A very common fish on the reef at depths ranging from 10 ft to 90 feet.
OBSERVATIONS: Can be seen in pairs or in large schools. This is naturally a very easy fish to approach, and when fed in popular snorkeling spots, these fish can get very bold.

COMMON NAME: Fourspot Butterflyfish

SCIENTIFIC NAME: *Chaetodon quadrimaculatus*
HAWAIIAN NAME: Lauhau
AVERAGE SIZE: 4 - 6 inches
DESCRIPTION AND DISTINCTIVE FEATURES:
Orange eye-bar bordered with black and blue followed by a yellow bar. Two white spots (each side) on dark part of upper part of body. Lower body yellow.
DIET: Coral polyps.
WHERE TO FIND THEM: On shallow outer reefs at depths ranging from 10 feet to 50 feet.

OBSERVATIONS: This species is easily approached by the unobtrusive diver.

COMMON NAME: Teardrop Butterflyfish

SCIENTIFIC NAME: *Chaetodon unimaculatus*

HAWAIIAN NAME: Kikākapu
AVERAGE SIZE: 5 - 7 inches
DESCRIPTION AND DISTINCTIVE FEATURES: The large black teardrop-like spot in the middle of the body makes it easy to identify this species. Also a broad black eye-bar and black vertical bar at base of tail.
DIET: Coral polyps, small crustaceans and other invertebrates, algae.
WHERE TO FIND THEM: Exposed reefs in depths from 20 -100 feet, but perhaps found most

often in the 40-60 foot range. Relatively uncommon.

OBSERVATIONS: Their reaction to divers ranges from skittish to quite approachable.

COMMON NAME: Forceps Butterflyfish

SCIENTIFIC NAME: *Forcipiger flavissimus*
HAWAIIAN NAME: Lau-wiliwili-nukunuku-ʻoiʻoi
AVERAGE SIZE: 4 - 6 inches
**DESCRIPTION AND DISTINCTIVE
FEATURES:** Almost identical to
Longnose Butterflyfish: yellow
body, long snout and black spot
on anal fin, but mouth opening
of this species is noticeably long.
DIET: Fish eggs, tube worms,
tubefeet of sea urchins, small
crustaceans.

WHERE TO FIND THEM: On seaward reefs in depths between 10 and 100 feet, occasionally in lagoons and bays.
OBSERVATIONS: Forceps butterflyfish use their extended snout to reach deep into crevices and coral to catch their prey. Usually allows divers to approach quite closely.

COMMON NAME: Longnose Butterflyfish

SCIENTIFIC NAME: *Forcipiger longirostris*
HAWAIIAN NAME: Lau-wiliwili-nukunuku-ʻoiʻoi
AVERAGE SIZE: 5 - 7 inches
**DESCRIPTION AND DISTINCTIVE
FEATURES:** Almost identical to
Forceps Butterflyfish, but this
species has a very small mouth
opening.
DIET: Fish eggs, tube worms,
tubefeet of urchins, small crustaceans.
WHERE TO FIND THEM: On seaward reefs in depths between 10
and 100 feet, favoring 60 feet and

below. Common only on the Big Island.
OBSERVATIONS: Longnose Butterflyfish use their extended snout to reach deep into crevices and coral to catch their prey. This species occasionally experiences a black phase which is seen quite commonly along the Kona Coast of the Big Island, but is rare elsewhere. There is no known explanation for this phase, since it does not appear related to feeding or reproduction. Fish placed into aquariums while in the black phase change back to their more common yellow phase.

COMMON NAME: Pyramid Butterflyfish

SCIENTIFIC NAME: *Hemitaurichthys polylepis*

AVERAGE SIZE: 5 inches
DESCRIPTION AND DISTINCTIVE FEATURES: Large white triangle on yellow body. Brownish tint on head.
DIET: Zooplankton.
WHERE TO FIND THEM: Most often seen in large congregations near current-swept dropoffs feeding in the water column in depths ranging from 20 to 100 feet or more.
OBSERVATIONS: Upon approach from open water the fish will often retreat to the cover of the reef. Here they usually allow divers to closely approach.

COMMON NAME: Thompson's Butterflyfish

SCIENTIFIC NAME: *Hemitaurichthys thompsoni*

AVERAGE SIZE: 5 - 7 inches
DESCRIPTION AND DISTINCTIVE FEATURES: Body entirely black-brown.
DIET: Zooplankton.
WHERE TO FIND THEM: In large schools feeding in the water column, most commonly below 60 feet. Not endemic to Hawaii, but only found in few locations beside Hawaii.

OBSERVATIONS: The only butterflyfish with drab colors. A very curious butterflyfish, which often approaches divers.

COMMON NAME: Pennant Butterflyfish

SCIENTIFIC NAME: *Heniochus diphreutes*
AVERAGE SIZE: 5 - 7 inches
DESCRIPTION AND DISTINCTIVE FEATURES: One dorsal spine and its membrane prolonged into a long "banner". Two broad black bars on body, yellow markings on base of pelvic fin, dorsal fin and tail. Often confused with the Moorish Idol, which has a longer snout, larger yellow patches and the exact opposite color pattern, and lacks visible scales.

DIET: Zooplankton.

WHERE TO FIND THEM: Most common in depths below 60 feet.

OBSERVATIONS: Often observed in schools feeding in the water column. Will react to divers very much like the Pyramid Butterflyfish. This species has also been known to clean other fishes.

Family: Moorish Idols - *Zanclidae*

Moorish Idols are the only member of their family (Zanclidae). Due to shape and color, this fish is often assumed to be in the angelfish or butterflyfish family, but is actually closely related to the surgeonfishes. Moorish Idols use their long snout to reach into crevices for food.

COMMON NAME: Moorish Idol

SCIENTIFIC NAME: *Zanclus cornutus*

HAWAIIAN NAME: Kihikihi

AVERAGE SIZE: 7 - 9 inches

DESCRIPTION AND DISTINCTIVE FEATURES: Often confused with Pennant Butterflyfish, but differs with a much narrower snout, more yellow markings on mid-body and black tail. Like the Pennant Butterflyfish, it has two broad black bars vertically over side of body. Scales are not visible.

DIET: Sponges, occasionally algae.

WHERE TO FIND THEM: A common fish on reefs ranging from the surge zone down to below 100 feet.

OBSERVATIONS: Often seen in groups of 3 to 5. Generally quite approachable.

Family: Surgeonfishes - *Acanthuridae*

The surgeonfish or tang family is named for the scalpel-like spines located on each side of the body near the base of the tail. Some of these fish have rigid spines while others can fold the spine almost flush against the body. These razor-sharp scalpel-like spines are used for defense and are quite effective. When hand-feeding, divers and snorkelers should be cautious to avoid being unintentionally sliced by these spines in a feeding frenzy. Most surgeonfishes feed on algae and inhabit shallow reefs. They arc commonly observed grazing the reef in large schools. Schooling provides them with greater protection and the ability to overwhelm territorial fishes such as the damselfish.

Reproduction is accomplished by the release of the eggs into the current, followed by fertilization by the male. Due to a long larval period, most species are widespread. At night surgeonfishes hide in the crevices of the reef.

Photography: During the day a 60mm macro lens is best to capture this medium-sized fish. At night, when dormant, it is possible with some of the species to (carefully) place a framer of a close-up kit around the animal. Note the different color patterns surgeonfishes display during the night.

COMMON NAME: Yellow Tang

SCIENTIFIC NAME: *Zebrasoma flavescens*
HAWAIIAN NAME: Lauʻi pala

AVERAGE SIZE: 4 - 6 inches
DESCRIPTION AND DISTINCTIVE FEATURES: White spine at base of tail, otherwise solid yellow body.
DIET: Filamentous algae.
WHERE TO FIND THEM: Occurs at depths between 15 and 100 feet, but most often observed on shallow reefs. This fish occurs in areas between Hawaii and Japan, but is only abundant in Hawaii.
OBSERVATIONS: Due to its bright colors and indifferent demeanor toward divers and snorkelers, this often is the first fish recognized by first-time snorkelers or divers in Hawaii. Heavily impacted by the aquarium fish trade.

COMMON NAME: Sailfin Tang

SCIENTIFIC NAME: *Zebrasoma veliferum*
HAWAIIAN NAME: Māneoneo
AVERAGE SIZE: 10 - 13 inches
DESCRIPTION AND DISTINCTIVE FEATURES: When erect, dorsal and anal fins are sail-like. Broad cream and narrow mustard vertical bars on side of body. Blue spine at base of tail. Yellow to mustard colored tail.

DIET: Filamentous algae.
WHERE TO FIND THEM: Most commonly seen in the surge zone amongst boulders. Seldom observed below 30 feet.
OBSERVATIONS: This species definitely likes to keep its distance from approaching snorkelers and divers.

COMMON NAME: Whitespotted Surgeonfish

SCIENTIFIC NAME: *Acanthurus guttatus*
HAWAIIAN NAME: ʻApi
AVERAGE SIZE: 9 - 11 inches
DESCRIPTION AND DISTINCTIVE FEATURES: Yellow pelvic fins. Two broad white bars on front part of body, white spots on rear body, white bar on tail.
DIET: Filamentous algae.
WHERE TO FIND THEM: Most commonly seen in the surge zone amongst boulders. Seldom observed below 30 feet.

OBSERVATIONS: Often seen in large schools grazing on algae. This is a skittish species which will flee into the turbulent surf when pursued. The white spots may provide camouflage, simulating the swirling white bubbles found in the surge zone.

COMMON NAME: Whitebar Surgeonfish

SCIENTIFIC NAME: *Acanthurus leucopareius*

HAWAIIAN NAME: Māikoiko
AVERAGE SIZE: 7 - 9 inches
DESCRIPTION AND DISTINCTIVE FEATURES: Broad white bar on side of head, followed by broad dark bar. White bar at base of tail. Gray-brown body with bluish spots.
DIET: Filamentous algae.
WHERE TO FIND THEM: Most commonly seen in the surge zone amongst boulders. Seldom observed below 30 feet.

OBSERVATIONS: Often seen in large schools grazing on algae. Relatively unconcerned about divers approach, but keeps its distance.

COMMON NAME: Lavender Tang

SCIENTIFIC NAME: *Acanthurus nigrofuscus*

HAWAIIAN NAME: Māʻiʻiʻi
AVERAGE SIZE: 5 inches
DESCRIPTION AND DISTINCTIVE FEATURES: Brownish-gray to lavender body, black spot at rear base of dorsal and anal fin. Head with yellow spots.
DIET: Filamentous algae.
WHERE TO FIND THEM: On shallow reefs, especially in or near the surge zone in boulder areas.

OBSERVATIONS: Allows divers to approach relatively close. A territorial species which will attack other herbivores.

COMMON NAME: Blue-lined Surgeonfish

SCIENTIFIC NAME: *Acanthurus nigroris*
HAWAIIAN NAME: Maiko
AVERAGE SIZE: 6 - 8 inches
DESCRIPTION AND DISTINCTIVE FEATURES: Similar to Black Tang, but lines more irregular and has

distinct blue lines at edge of all fins and tail.

DIET: Filamentous algae and detritus.

WHERE TO FIND THEM: A common fish found on the coral reef at various depths.

OBSERVATIONS: This tang tends to prefer to keep its distance. May display a dark or light color phase at will.

COMMON NAME: Goldring Surgeonfish

SCIENTIFIC NAME: *Ctenochaetus strigosus*

HAWAIIAN NAME: Kole
AVERAGE SIZE: 4 - 6 inches
DESCRIPTION AND DISTINCTIVE FEATURES: Similar to Black Tang, but with golden iris and golden ring around eye and lines not as narrow.
DIET: Detritus.
WHERE TO FIND THEM: This is one of the most common fishes in coral-rich bays and reefs, at depths ranging from just below the surface to 100 feet.

OBSERVATIONS: Usually unafraid and allows divers to get close. May occasionally be seen schooling by the hundreds.

COMMON NAME: Black Tang

SCIENTIFIC NAME: *Ctenochaetus hawaiiensis*

AVERAGE SIZE: 8 - 10 inches
DESCRIPTION AND DISTINCTIVE FEATURES: Black body with innumerable very fine lines along body and all fins. (Juveniles see chevron tang)
DIET: Detritus.
WHERE TO FIND THEM: On coral reefs normally above 50 feet, but can be occasionally be found at greater depths.
OBSERVATIONS: This is a common fish, which tends to be quite approachable.

COMMON NAME: Chevron Tang

SCIENTIFIC NAME: *Ctenochaetus hawaiiensis*
AVERAGE SIZE: 4 inches
DESCRIPTION AND DISTINCTIVE FEATURES:
Bright orange body with distinct chevron
pattern. (Adults see Black Tang)
DIET: Detritus.
WHERE TO FIND THEM: Singularly within the
protection of Finger Coral at depths below
50 feet.
OBSERVATIONS: This is the juvenile only.
(Adult Chevron Tangs are referred to as
Black Tangs)

COMMON NAME: Achilles Tang

SCIENTIFIC NAME: *Acanthurus achilles*
HAWAIIAN NAME: Pāku'iku'i
AVERAGE SIZE: 7 - 10 inches
**DESCRIPTION AND DISTINCTIVE
FEATURES:** Large orange spot
on side of rear body, orange
tail. Black body, with some
white markings.
DIET: Filamentous and small
fleshy algae.
WHERE TO FIND THEM: Most
commonly seen in the surge

zone amongst boulders. Seldom observed below 30 feet.
OBSERVATIONS: This species definitely likes to keep its distance from approaching
snorkelers and divers.

COMMON NAME: Goldrim Tang

SCIENTIFIC NAME: *Acanthurus
nigricans*
AVERAGE SIZE: 6 - 7 inches
**DESCRIPTION AND DISTINCTIVE
FEATURES:** White rim under
eye, white stripe near snout,
white tail with yellow stripe,
yellow spine at base of tail, fins
feature yellow and blue on
edges, body black.

DIET: Filamentous algae.

WHERE TO FIND THEM: A rare fish in Hawaii, most often seen in the surge zone amongst boulders.

OBSERVATIONS: This species is not too afraid, but definitely likes to keep its distance from approaching snorkelers and divers. Sometimes hybridizes with Achilles Tang.

COMMON NAME: Orangeband Surgeonfish

SCIENTIFIC NAME: *Acanthurus olivaceus*
HAWAIIAN NAME: Na'ena'e

AVERAGE SIZE: 12 inches

DESCRIPTION AND DISTINCTIVE FEATURES: Orange band with blue trim behind eye. May change body color, but is frequently seen with a color pattern which is of a light grey at front part of body, changing abruptly to black at rear of body.

DIET: Detritus, filamentous algae.

WHERE TO FIND THEM: At depths below 20 feet in sandy and rubble areas, generally near the reef.

OBSERVATIONS: This species often responds indifferent toward divers, thus allowing them to approach closely. Sometimes observed in schools.

COMMON NAME: Orangespine Surgeonfish

SCIENTIFIC NAME: *Naso lituratus*
HAWAIIAN NAME: Umaumalei

AVERAGE SIZE: 10 - 12 inches

DESCRIPTION AND DISTINCTIVE FEATURES: Yellow band from snout to eye. Orange lips, two orange spines at base of tail.

DIET: Leafy brown algae.

WHERE TO FIND THEM: In areas with coral, rock or rubble at a depths below 10 feet.

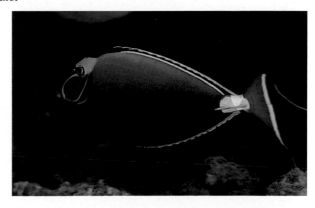

OBSERVATIONS: This species often responds indifferent toward divers, thus allowing them to approach closely. Sometimes observed in schools. Males have greatly elongated caudal rays.

COMMON NAME: Eye-striped Surgeonfish

SCIENTIFIC NAME: *Acanthurus dussumieri*
HAWAIIAN NAME: Palani
AVERAGE SIZE: 18 inches
DESCRIPTION AND DISTINCTIVE FEATURES:
Yellow band over eye, white spine at base of tail, two yellow markings on tail. Fine, irregular blue lines on face and body.
DIET: Filamentous and blue-green algae.
WHERE TO FIND THEM: On the reef or near rocks at depths below 25 feet.
OBSERVATIONS: This tang often allows divers to get very close.

COMMON NAME: Yellowfin Surgeonfish

SCIENTIFIC NAME: *Acanthurus xanthopterus*
HAWAIIAN NAME: Pualu
AVERAGE SIZE: 18 inches
DESCRIPTION AND DISTINCTIVE FEATURES:
Fine, irregular blue lines on face and body. Yellow band over eye, yellow pelvic fins, sometimes has white band at base of tail. Spine at base of tail is black.
DIET: Filamentous and blue-green algae.
WHERE TO FIND THEM: Most commonly below 50 feet above the reef or on sand areas at times far from the reef.
OBSERVATIONS: Not as common and usually doesn't allow divers to get a close as Eye-stripe Surgeonfish.

COMMON NAME: Bluespine Surgeonfish

SCIENTIFIC NAME: *Naso unicornis*

HAWAIIAN NAME: Kala

AVERAGE SIZE: 15 - 20 inches

DESCRIPTION AND DISTINCTIVE FEATURES: Bony unicorn-like horn in front of eyes, two blue spines at base of tail.

DIET: Leafy brown algae.

WHERE TO FIND THEM: Most commonly seen in the surge zone, but also found on deeper seaward reefs.

OBSERVATIONS: This fish generally prefers to keep its distance from divers and snorkelers.

COMMON NAME: Thompson's Surgeonfish

SCIENTIFIC NAME: *Acanthurus thompsoni*

AVERAGE SIZE: 5 - 7 inches

DESCRIPTION AND DISTINCTIVE FEATURES: Body uniformly grayish to dark brown. Small black spot between dorsal fin and tail. Tail crescent shaped.

DIET: Zooplankton.

WHERE TO FIND THEM: Well above the reef (midwater) in depths below 40 feet.

OBSERVATIONS: Encountered in schools feeding above the reef. Rarely allows divers to approach closely.

COMMON NAME: Paletail or Spotted Unicornfish

SCIENTIFIC NAME: *Naso brevirostris*
HAWAIIAN NAME: Kala lōlō
AVERAGE SIZE: 12 - 15 inches
DESCRIPTION AND DISTINCTIVE FEATURES: Brown body with numerous vertical lines. Able to take on a color phase with front body very pale. Pale tail. Distinctive long horn in adults.
DIET: Zooplankton.
WHERE TO FIND THEM: Usually seen feeding in groups in the water column above exposed reefs.

OBSERVATIONS: Juveniles lack the prominent horn found in adults. Generally this unicornfish does not allow divers to approach very closely.

COMMON NAME: Convict Tang   E

SCIENTIFIC NAME: *Acanthurus triostegus sandvicensis*
HAWAIIAN NAME: Manini
AVERAGE SIZE: 4 - 6 inches
DESCRIPTION AND DISTINCTIVE FEATURES: Six narrow black bars vertically over head, body and base of tail.
DIET: Filamentous algae.
WHERE TO FIND THEM: Usually in very shallow boulder areas, but may occur at depths down to 100 feet. The subspecies is endemic to Hawaii.

OBSERVATIONS: A very common fish in Hawaii, which is observed grazing the reef and boulder areas in the surge zone in large schools. This allows them to overwhelm territorial fish, such as damselfishes, when grazing.

CHAPTER TWO

Small Ovals and Discs

Angelfishes - Damselfishes

Small Ovals and Discs

Angelfishes - Damselfishes

Family: Angelfishes - *Pomacanthidae*

Often confused for butterflyfishes, angelfishes can be distinguished by the spine located on the lower gill cover. Although angelfishes in other parts of the Indo-Pacific and the Caribbean can grow to a substantial size, Hawaii's species are smaller and tend to be quite skittish. They live in haremic social systems, with each male defending two to five females. Being territorial grazers, they utilize their brushlike teeth to feed on algae and sponges. Spawning is paired and usually occurs at sunset.

Photography: Since most angelfishes are quite shy, patience is required to photograph them. Just remain in their territory for a while and let them get used to you. Upon a diver's approach they commonly dart into the cover of Finger Coral, but soon curiosity takes over and they reappear. They generally play a game of "now you see me, now you don't" with the photographer. As soon as you manage to set your focus, they dart into protection again, and just when you're ready to give up, they return into the open, just a few inches from the last location, and of course just out of your focus range, while looking all innocent and ready to model for you. This game may go on for a while, but with patience you will eventually get your shot! Photographing angelfish requires a housed system with a 60-105mm macro lens. It is virtually impossible to get them to jump through the hoop (framer).

COMMON NAME: Flame Angelfish

SCIENTIFIC NAME: *Centropyge loriculus*

AVERAGE SIZE: 2 - 3 inches

DESCRIPTION AND DISTINCTIVE FEATURES: Easily recognized by its spectacular flame red body color, black vertical bars on sides of body and blue markings on anal and dorsal fin.

DIET: Filamentous algae.

WHERE TO FIND THEM: Most often in areas of rich coral growth, especially Finger Coral gardens at depths between 40 to 70 feet, although they do occur shallower and deeper. Since this is a highly-prized aquarium fish, and regularly collected for this purpose, your best chances to see this spectacular fish in its natural environment is in marine preserves, such as Kealakekua Bay or remote dive sites.

OBSERVATIONS: If you spot a Flame Angel Fish, your best bet is to remain very still and non-threatening, and if necessary, back up a few feet. Once the fish feels threatened (watched), it will often begin to swim a distinctive pattern in and around the surrounding coral, periodically pausing for a split second to check out the intruder (diver). It is during this pause you get your best look (photograph) of this evasive fish.

COMMON NAME: Potter's Angelfish   E

SCIENTIFIC NAME: *Centropyge potteri*

AVERAGE SIZE: 3 - 5 inches

DESCRIPTION AND DISTINCTIVE FEATURES: Orange head and upper body, rest of body blue. Dark, irregular lines cover sides of body.

DIET: Filamentous algae.

WHERE TO FIND THEM: On the open reef in depths from 15 -100 feet. A common fish which is endemic to the Hawaiian Islands.

OBSERVATIONS: A skittish angelfish which is frequently seen, darting in and out of the coral. To best observe this fish, remain motionless and practice patience.

COMMON NAME: Dusky or Fisher's Angelfish   E

SCIENTIFIC NAME: *Centropyge fisheri*

AVERAGE SIZE: 3 inches

DESCRIPTION AND DISTINCTIVE FEATURES: Coloration may vary, but base color is orange, with a more-or-less blue overlaying sheen to it. Tail tends to be yellow. Iridescent blue rim on pelvic, dorsal and anal fins.

DIET: Filamentous algae.

WHERE TO FIND THEM: Generally in areas with rich coral growth at depths below 60 feet. Endemic to Hawaii.

OBSERVATIONS: Generally found living in small colonies of five to ten individuals, these small angelfishes are commonly seen darting in and out of protective cover while feeding. They tend to be very skittish and are difficult to get close to. Remain still and be patient and their curiosity will get the better of them.

COMMON NAME: Bandit Angelfish   E

SCIENTIFIC NAME: *Desmoholacanthus arcuatus*

AVERAGE SIZE: 5 - 7 inches

DESCRIPTION AND DISTINCTIVE FEATURES: Broad black stripe along side of body, covering eye. Upper body greyish, lower body bright white. Black bands on anal fin and tail.

DIET: Sponges.

WHERE TO FIND THEM: On the reef, often along steeper walls. Usually encountered deeper than 80 feet, it occasionally ventures into areas as shallow as 30 feet or more. Endemic to Hawaii.

OBSERVATIONS: This is a free-roaming species which is quite curious and freely approaches divers. Common to see singularly.

COMMON NAME: Masked Angelfish   E

SCIENTIFIC NAME: *Genicanthus personatus*

© MIKE SEVERNS

AVERAGE SIZE: 8 - 9 inches

DESCRIPTION AND DISTINCTIVE FEATURES: Female white with black patch over eyes and forehead and broad black bar on tail. Male white with orange face and fins. Tail has broad black bar like female.

DIET: Zooplankton.

WHERE TO FIND THEM: This species is endemic to Hawaii. In the main islands it is rare and occurs mostly at depths below 300 feet. It is more common in the Northwest Hawaiian Islands in as little as 60 feet.

OBSERVATIONS: This species feeds on zooplankton while hovering above the reef adjacent to current-swept dropoffs.

Male

© MIKE SEVERNS

Family: Damselfishes - *Pomacentridae*

This family is well-represented on Hawaiian reefs and several species may be encountered during a dive. Damselfishes protect their territory from intruders, and some species are even bold enough to charge at divers. Luckily they are too small to harm humans. Before reproducing, the female damselfish will prepare a coral or rocky area to lay her eggs. Once the eggs are laid, the male fertilizes them and guards them until hatching. A prime example is the Sergeant Major, which will ferociously charge and warn off any intruder.

Photography: Due to their territorial and often bold behavior, it's generally not too difficult to capture damselfishes when using a housed camera/macro lens or a close-up kit for the Nikonos without the framer.

COMMON NAME: Hawaiian Sergeant Major   E

SCIENTIFIC NAME: *Abudefduf abdominalis*

HAWAIIAN NAME: Mamo
AVERAGE SIZE: 7 - 9 inches
DESCRIPTION AND DISTINCTIVE FEATURES: Five black bars, yellow tint only as juveniles, fades as they grow into a greenish-white. Black marking on anal fin.
DIET: Zooplankton, occasionally algae.
WHERE TO FIND THEM: From the surface down to 100 feet, often seen in large schools feeding in the water column above the reef, or close to the reef when guarding eggs. Endemic to Hawaii.

OBSERVATIONS: Sergeant Majors aggregate in schools and lay their eggs as purplish egg masses on the reef, often on Plate Coral. They will protect their eggs ferociously against predators such as butterflyfishes, wrasses and other Mamo. They are also known to boldly approach divers while attempting to chase them away.

COMMON NAME: Blackspot Damselfish

SCIENTIFIC NAME: *Abudefduf sordidus*
HAWAIIAN NAME: Kupipi
AVERAGE SIZE: 7 - 9 inches
**DESCRIPTION AND DISTINC-
TIVE FEATURES:** Six dark
bars, that can lighten or dark-
en. Black spot at base of tail.
DIET: Algae and small crus-
taceans.
WHERE TO FIND THEM: In the

surge zone among rocks and boulders.
OBSERVATIONS: A very territorial damselfish that readily approaches divers.

COMMON NAME: Chocolate-dip Damselfish   E

SCIENTIFIC NAME: *Chromis hanui*
AVERAGE SIZE: 2 - 3 inches
**DESCRIPTION AND DISTINCTIVE
FEATURES:** Black spot at base of
pectoral fins. White tail.
DIET: Zooplankton.
WHERE TO FIND THEM: Close to
the reef, as shallow as 5 feet
down to 130 feet or more. This
species only exists in Hawaii.
OBSERVATIONS: If you remain

quiet, this damselfish often becomes curious and approaches divers. May exhibit an
unusual color pattern of light and dark brown, with a bright blue iris.

COMMON NAME: Whitetail Chromis

SCIENTIFIC NAME: *Chromis leucura*

AVERAGE SIZE: 2 inches
**DESCRIPTION AND DISTINCTIVE FEA-
TURES:** White tail, yellow spot on pectoral fins, yellow pectoral fins, and blue
line around eyes and edge of dorsal and
anal fin.
DIET: Zooplankton.
WHERE TO FIND THEM: On the reef, generally below 80 feet.
OBSERVATIONS: This rare species is often
confused with the Chocolate-dip Dam-
selfish. Like most damselfishes, it is relatively easy to get close to.

COMMON NAME: Agile Chromis

SCIENTIFIC NAME: *Chromis agilis*

AVERAGE SIZE: 2 - 4 inches

DESCRIPTION AND DISTINCTIVE FEATURES: Pink to lavender sheen on face and chest. Black spot at base of pectoral fins.

DIET: Zooplankton.

WHERE TO FIND THEM: On the reef from 20 feet down to 100 feet and deeper. More common on the leeward sides of the islands.

OBSERVATIONS: If you remain still, Agile Chromis often become curious and approach quite closely to divers. These fish are generally found in loosely associated schools.

COMMON NAME: Oval Chromis   E

SCIENTIFIC NAME: *Chromis ovalis*

Juvenile

AVERAGE SIZE: 4 - 7 inches

DESCRIPTION AND DISTINCTIVE FEATURES: Bronze body, pink lips, sometimes has blue sheen on tail. Capable of displaying a steel gray color phase when feeding.

DIET: Zooplankton.

WHERE TO FIND THEM: Often seen feeding in the water column in schools, but never far from the protection of the reef. Endemic to Hawaii.

OBSERVATIONS: A common fish, often observed in schools. Sometimes difficult to get close to.

Adult

COMMON NAME: Pacific Gregory

SCIENTIFIC NAME: *Stegastes fasciolatus*
AVERAGE SIZE: 3 - 5 inches
DESCRIPTION AND DISTINCTIVE FEATURES:
Yellow iris, sometimes has black
blotches.
DIET: Filamentous algae.
WHERE TO FIND THEM: On shallow
reef flats, often in the surge zone.

OBSERVATIONS: This pugnacious damselfish can be observed defending its territory
against other algae-eating fish and is known to even boldly approach divers, in an
attempt to chase them away. Look for a "garden" of greenish filamentous algae which
it carefully maintains.

COMMON NAME: Blue-eye Damselfish

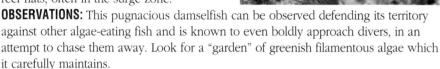

SCIENTIFIC NAME: *Plectroglyphidodon johnstonianus*

AVERAGE SIZE: 3 - 4 inches
**DESCRIPTION AND DISTINCTIVE
FEATURES:** Blue iris, blue marking on dorsal fin.
DIET: Coral polyps.
WHERE TO FIND THEM: As shallow as 15 feet, but more often in
deeper water, associated with
live branching coral.

OBSERVATIONS: This fish can be seen actively swimming among the branches of
Antler and Cauliflower Corals. Generally allows divers to approach quite closely
before it darts into the protection of the coral.

COMMON NAME: Brighteye Damselfish

SCIENTIFIC NAME: *Plectroglyphidodon imparipennis*

AVERAGE SIZE: 2 inches
DESCRIPTION AND DISTINCTIVE FEATURES:
Grayish body, yellowish at base of tail, yellow
tail. Black bar through pupil, iris bright silver.
DIET: Small invertebrates.
WHERE TO FIND THEM: Shallow reefs and tide
pools with good water circulation.
OBSERVATIONS: Often eyes divers curiously,
but immediately flees when diver approaches.

COMMON NAME: Blackfin Chromis

SCIENTIFIC NAME: *Chromis vanderbilti*
AVERAGE SIZE: 2 inches
DESCRIPTION AND DISTINCTIVE FEATURES:
Rows of blue spots along side of body.
Blue markings on outer edge of fins.
Orange stripe on dorsal fin. Distinctive
black stripe on tail.
DIET: Zooplankton, occasionally algae.
WHERE TO FIND THEM: Commonly seen
hovering near rocky outcrops from 10 to
60 feet.

OBSERVATIONS: Occurs in aggregations. Allows divers to get quite close, but is difficult to photograph since these fish seem to be constantly in motion.

COMMON NAME: Threespot Chromis   E

SCIENTIFIC NAME: *Chromis verater*
AVERAGE SIZE: 7 - 9 inches
DESCRIPTION AND DISTINCTIVE
FEATURES: Three white spots on
black body. Body color may
become faint to light grey, spots
may darken.
DIET: Zooplankton.
WHERE TO FIND THEM: Can be
found on the reef at depths below
30 feet adjacent to dropoffs, most
common at 50 feet or more.
Endemic to Hawaii.

Juvenile

OBSERVATIONS: Can be
observed singularly or in
small, loose schools.

Adult

COMMON NAME: Whitespot Damselfish
or Hawaiian Dascyllus

E

SCIENTIFIC NAME: *Dascyllus albisella*

Juvenile

HAWAIIAN NAME: 'Aloʻiloʻi
AVERAGE SIZE: 3 - 5 inches
DESCRIPTION AND DISTINCTIVE FEATURES:
During daylight a whitish body, with only the

Adult

fins, tail and head remaining black. At night a black body with a single white spot.

DIET: Zooplankton.

WHERE TO FIND THEM: From the surface down to 100 feet or more, generally associated with Antler Coral. Endemic to Hawaii.

OBSERVATIONS: A very territorial damselfish, which is commonly observed hovering above Antler Coral. As soon as danger is detected, these damselfishes dart into the protection of the coral branches. If you remain motionless, they will often leave the coral again and return into their hovering position in the open. The juveniles generally show similar behavior, but associate with Cauliflower Coral.

SMALL OVALS AND DISCS

40

CHAPTER THREE

Swims with Pectoral Fins

Wrasses - Hogfish - Parrotfishes

Swims with Pectoral Fins

Wrasses - Hogfish - Parrotfishes

Family: Wrasses and Hogfish - *Labridae*

The wrasse family is a very diverse category of fish with an interesting and complex social structure and brilliant color patterns that can change with age or sex. Wrasses are generally classified by their various life phases, including the initial, the intermediate or adult, and the terminal phase. While some wrasses hatch as males and remain male during every phase, many other individuals begin life as females and later experience a sex change, transforming into "supermales". Supermales are usually the most brilliantly colored of the species, which dominate a territory. If a supermale dies, the next largest wrasse, male or female, quickly changes into a supermale. If a more controlling supermale is introduced to the population, other supermales may even reverse back to their initial phase.

Wrasses are generally carnivorous, feeding on invertebrates or smaller fishes. There are some that feed on zooplankton while others are cleaners that feed on parasites from other fish, such as the cleaner wrasse. It is common to see different species of wrasses working together while feeding in rubble areas. Their predominant colors are the greens, blues and yellows. Most wrasses have noticeable front teeth that are used to capture prey. Wrasses forage for food during the day and become inactive at night, burying themselves under the sand for protection, with the exception of the cleaner wrasse, which instead forms a mucous cocoon similar to the parrotfish.

Photography: Because of their habit to bury themselves under the sand at night, most wrasses can only be photographed during the day. Probably the most challenging fish family to photograph, wrasses are very fast swimmers, with many of them being quite shy. Many also live in the surge zone which compounds the problem. When hand-fed, some bold species, such as the Saddle Wrasse may be coached into the framer of a macro kit, but normally a 60mm or 105mm macro lens is necessary to photograph them.

COMMON NAME: Surge Wrasse

SCIENTIFIC NAME: *Thalassoma purpureum*

Male

HAWAIIAN NAME: Hou
AVERAGE SIZE: 10 - 15 inches
DESCRIPTION AND DISTINCTIVE FEATURES: The males have a beautiful color pattern with three pink stripes connected by three rows of small pink bars on green body. Pink facial lines partially radiating from eye. Females (initial phase) have brown stripes and bars on greenish body.

Female

DIET: Crabs, other small invertebrates, and fishes.

WHERE TO FIND THEM: On rocky areas or very shallow reef in the surge zone, often only a few feet deep.

OBSERVATIONS: Due to its preference for rough shallow waters, this species is most often seen by snorkelers rather than divers. This is a fast-swimming wrasse which, along with the surge, makes it a very challenging subject for snorkelers and divers. Males are very uncommon in Hawaii, and females look almost exactly like the initial phase Christmas Wrasse.

COMMON NAME: Christmas Wrasse

SCIENTIFIC NAME: *Thalassoma trilobatum*

Female

HAWAIIAN NAME: 'Awela
AVERAGE SIZE: 8 - 12 inches
DESCRIPTION AND DISTINCTIVE FEATURES: The males have a brilliant color pattern, consisting of two rows of rectangular turquoise bars on salmon red body. Blue markings on all fins. Females (initial phase) have greenish body with irregular rows of brown spots and stripes. Irregular spots and lines on face.

DIET: Small invertebrates.

WHERE TO FIND THEM: On rocky areas or very shallow reefs in the surge zone, often only a few feet deep.

OBSERVATIONS: Due to its preference for rough shallow waters, this species is most often seen by snorkelers rather than divers. This is

Male

another fast-swimming wrasse which, along with the surge, makes it a very challenging subject for snorkelers and divers. Much more common than the Surge Wrasse, females of both species are virtually identical in appearance.

COMMON NAME: Fivestripe Wrasse

SCIENTIFIC NAME: *Thalassoma quinquevittatum*
AVERAGE SIZE: 4 - 6 inches
DESCRIPTION AND DISTINCTIVE FEATURES: A very attractive color pattern with two magenta stripes connected by a row of magenta bars on green body. The head has distinct green lines on magenta.

DIET: Small crustaceans and mollusks.
WHERE TO FIND THEM: On shallow reef flats in or near the surge zone in very shallow water. Rare in Hawaii.
OBSERVATIONS: A fast swimmer that rarely allows divers to approach closely.

COMMON NAME: Belted Wrasse   E

SCIENTIFIC NAME: *Stethojulis balteata*

Male

HAWAIIAN NAME: ʻŌmaka
AVERAGE SIZE: 4 - 5 inches
DESCRIPTION AND DISTINCTIVE FEATURES: Males have distinct blue horizontal lines along green head through eye and green body. Orange horizontal stripe along side of body.

Orange dorsal fin. Females are gray peppered with white. Orange mark above pectoral fin. Two black spots ringed with white near tail.

Female

DIET: Small crustaceans and mollusks.
WHERE TO FIND THEM: A common fish on shallow reefs, especially in the surge zone. Endemic to Hawaii.
OBSERVATIONS: A very fast swimmer which tends to favor the surge zone, hence making it difficult for divers to get close.

COMMON NAME: Ornate Wrasse

SCIENTIFIC NAME: *Halichoeres ornatissimus*
HAWAIIAN NAME: ʻŌhua
AVERAGE SIZE: 4 - 6 inches
DESCRIPTION AND DISTINCTIVE FEATURES: Males have a red body with rows of green squarish spots. The head has distinct turquoise stripes. Females have

Juvenile

(vertical sidebar text) SWIMS WITH PECTORAL FINS

neon green markings on a reddish brown background.

DIET: Small crustaceans and mollusks.

WHERE TO FIND THEM: Between 5 - 70 feet on the reef, remaining close to the bottom.

OBSERVATIONS: A fast swimmer which tends to be quite shy, but sometimes allows divers to approach.

COMMON NAME: Elegant Coris　　　　E

SCIENTIFIC NAME: *Coris venusta*
AVERAGE SIZE: 5 - 6 inches
DESCRIPTION AND DISTINCTIVE FEATURES: Female yellowish green with reddish stripes on yellow head and front of body. Rear part of body has irregular spots. Males are greener on body and have less stripes. Head red with green stripes.

DIET: Small invertebrates.
WHERE TO FIND THEM: In shallow areas with sand and rubble bottom. Endemic to Hawaii.
OBSERVATIONS: A fast swimmer which is quite skittish when approached. This fish requires a lot of patience to get close to.

COMMON NAME: Yellowtail Coris

SCIENTIFIC NAME: *Coris gaimard*
HAWAIIAN NAME: Hinālea ʻakilolo
AVERAGE SIZE: 12 - 15 inches

DESCRIPTION AND DISTINCTIVE FEATURES: The juvenile is bright orange with several white bars edged with black. The adult is noted for the brilliant blue spots on the body, the bright yellow tail and the distinct green stripes over the orange head.

DIET: Crabs, hermit crabs, mollusks.
WHERE TO FIND THEM: In shallow to deep areas with rubble bottom. Look for them in rubble areas within reef structures.

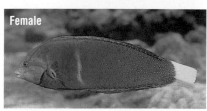

OBSERVATIONS: The juvenile is often confused with the South Pacific clownfish.

Clownfishes or anemonefishes don't exist in Hawaii, and the only thing the juvenile

Yellowtail Coris and the clownfish have in common are the similar color patterns. Their behavioral traits are also very different. Juveniles initially react skittish toward the approaching diver, but if the diver remains still, they soon become curious and emerge from their hideout. The adults vary from shy to bulletproof.

COMMON NAME: Sunset Wrasse

SCIENTIFIC NAME: *Thalassoma lutescens*

AVERAGE SIZE: 6 - 8 inches

DESCRIPTION AND DISTINCTIVE FEATURES: In the initial phase this wrasse has an underlying yellow beneath patterns. In the terminal phase note green lines on reddish head, while the body is green with vertical purple lines.

DIET: Crabs and other small invertebrates.

WHERE TO FIND THEM: On the reef and rubbly areas. Similar to the Saddle Wrasse, but quite uncommon.

OBSERVATIONS: May occasionally be seen schooling with the Saddle Wrasse, it has been known to hybridize with it.

COMMON NAME: Saddle Wrasse   E

SCIENTIFIC NAME: *Thalassoma duperrey*

HAWAIIAN NAME: Hinālea lauwili

AVERAGE SIZE: 7 - 10 inches

DESCRIPTION AND DISTINCTIVE FEATURES: Blue head, followed by an orange bar wrapping around body followed by a faint white bar. The rest of the body is a dull green.

DIET: Crabs and other small invertebrates.

WHERE TO FIND THEM: In rubble and sand areas near the reef. This species is one of the most common fishes on the reef and endemic to Hawaii.

OBSERVATIONS: This wrasse is quite bold and doesn't hesitate with divers, especially in areas where fish have been fed. The Saddle Wrasse also cleans other fishes and Green Sea Turtles.

Hybrid of Sunset Wrasse and Saddle Wrasse. These two species are known to occasionally crossbreed.

COMMON NAME: Blacktail or Old Woman Wrasse   E

SCIENTIFIC NAME: *Thalassoma ballieui*

Juvenile

HAWAIIAN NAME: Hinālea luahine
AVERAGE SIZE: 10 - 12 inches
DESCRIPTION AND DISTINCTIVE FEATURES: One of the least attractively hued wrasses. Body color varies from light grey (terminal male phase) to dark brown (initial phase) with yellow markings on eye, pelvic and dorsal fin. Broad black band on base of tail, which is not always visible. Juveniles are bright yellowish-green.

DIET: Small urchins, small fishes, crabs and a variety of small crustaceans.

WHERE TO FIND THEM: On the reef between 10 and 80 feet. Only found in Hawaii.

OBSERVATIONS: This aggressive feeder and active swimmer is generally unafraid and often allows close approach.

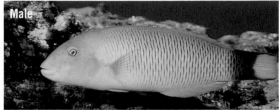
Male

Female

SWIMS WITH PECTORAL FINS

COMMON NAME: Ringtail Wrasse

SCIENTIFIC NAME: *Cheilinus unifasciatus*

Juvenile

HAWAIIAN NAME: Po'ou
AVERAGE SIZE: 12 - 15 inches
DESCRIPTION AND DISTINCTIVE FEATURES: This species is capable of fast color changes, resulting in variable color patterns. The white band around its body near the tail appears to be permanent. The face features irregular lines which may also vary in color.

DIET: Small fishes, crabs and urchins.

WHERE TO FIND THEM: On coral reefs at depths ranging from 30 to 100 feet.

OBSERVATIONS: A curious wrasse which sometimes approaches divers.

Adult Male

COMMON NAME: Rockmover

SCIENTIFIC NAME: *Novaculichthys taeniourus*

Juvenile

AVERAGE SIZE: 10 - 12 inches
DESCRIPTION AND DISTINCTIVE FEATURES:
Body black with vertical rows of rectangular white spots. Whitish face with dark lines radiating from eye, giving it a star-like appearance. White band on tail.
DIET: Small invertebrates, such as brittle stars, sea urchins, and mollusks.
WHERE TO FIND THEM: In areas with sand, rubble or loose coral at depths ranging from 10 - 70 feet.

OBSERVATIONS: Rockmovers often follow divers, hoping they will disturb the bottom to facilitate the food search. Generally they allow divers to approach quite easily. The juvenile is known as the "Dragon Wrasse" and is commonly observed mimicking a piece of algae.

© RAY MOCK

Adult

This adult Rockmover is still relatively young. As they mature their color pattern looses its brilliance.

COMMON NAME: Bird Wrasse

SCIENTIFIC NAME: *Gomphosus varius*
HAWAIIAN NAME: Hinālea i'iwi (male)
Hinālea 'akilolo (female)
AVERAGE SIZE: 8 - 12 inches
DESCRIPTION AND DISTINCTIVE FEATURES: Initial phase (females) has white front shading into black

Juvenile

at rear of body. Males have a greenish-blue body. The most distinctive feature is the prolonged snout in both phases.
DIET: Small crustaceans, brittle stars, mollusks.
WHERE TO FIND THEM: An obvious and common inhabitant of the reef at depths ranging from 15 - 100 feet.

Female

Male

OBSERVATIONS: These fish can be observed utilizing their long snouts to probe into crevices and coral for food. This is a very active wrasse, thus making it very difficult to get close to.

COMMON NAME: Psychedelic Wrasse

SCIENTIFIC NAME: *Anampses chrysocephalus*

Female

AVERAGE SIZE: 5 - 7 inches
DESCRIPTION AND DISTINCTIVE FEATURES:
Females are recognized by brilliant white spots over black body, white band at base of tail, red tail. Males stand out with bright red heads

Male

with blue irregular lines and an otherwise dull-looking body.
DIET: Small invertebrates.
WHERE TO FIND THEM: On the reef below 50 feet. Usually stays close to the reef. An uncommon species that is only found in Hawaii.
OBSERVATIONS: A very shy fish that is difficult to approach. Often occurs in groups. Since this species is quite rare, it is worth being patient and remaining still for a while. You never know when you'll see them again.

COMMON NAME: Pearl Wrasse

SCIENTIFIC NAME: *Anampses cuvier*

© KEOKI STENDER

HAWAIIAN NAME: Opule
AVERAGE SIZE: 12 inches
DESCRIPTION AND DISTINCTIVE FEATURES: Body of females brown with lower part being red. Brilliant white spots over body. Males are green with fine blue lines, and red marks on the face.
DIET: Small invertebrates.

WHERE TO FIND THEM: In shallow reef and boulder areas, often in or near the surge zone. Endemic to Hawaii.
OBSERVATIONS: Due to its skittish conduct and preference for very shallow water, this wrasse often goes unnoticed.

COMMON NAME: Eight-line Wrasse

SCIENTIFIC NAME: *Pseudocheilinus octotaenia*
AVERAGE SIZE: 3 - 5 inches
DESCRIPTION AND DISTINCTIVE FEATURES: Eight horizontal black lines

along reddish body. Yellow markings on dorsal and anal fin and on tail.

DIET: Very small crustaceans and mollusks

WHERE TO FIND THEM: On reefs at depths ranging from 10 - 100 feet. Species moves along the bottom, in and among the Finger Coral and small coral formations in rubble areas.

OBSERVATIONS: Due to its habit of staying close to the bottom, smaller size and initial shyness, this species is often overlooked. If you remain in one place looking for this fish, it often becomes curious and may approach you.

COMMON NAME: Fourline Wrasse

SCIENTIFIC NAME: *Pseudocheilinus tetrataenia*
AVERAGE SIZE: 1 - 2 inches
DESCRIPTION AND DISTINCTIVE FEATURES:
Brownish body with four blue lines on upper body and iridescent blue line on lower half of body. Red markings on eye and fins.

DIET: Very small crustaceans and mollusks.
WHERE TO FIND THEM: On reefs at depths ranging from 20 - 100 feet. Species moves along the bottom in and among the Finger Coral and small coral formations in rubble areas.

OBSERVATIONS: Due to its habit of staying close to the bottom, smaller size and extreme shyness, this species is often overlooked.

COMMON NAME: Disappearing Wrasse

SCIENTIFIC NAME: *Pseudocheilinus evanidus*
AVERAGE SIZE: 2 - 3 inches

DESCRIPTION AND DISTINCTIVE FEATURES: Brick red body with many fine white lines. Prominent white line on face below eye. Chin and lips are yellow.
DIET: Very small crustaceans and mollusks
WHERE TO FIND THEM: On reefs at depths ranging from 30 - 130 feet or more. Species rests on the bottom in and among the Finger Coral and rubble areas.

OBSERVATIONS: Due to its habit of staying close to the bottom, smaller size and initial shyness, this species is often overlooked. If you remain in one place looking for this fish, it often becomes curious and may approach you. More common in sand and rubble areas on the reef slope.

COMMON NAME: Hawaiian Cleaner Wrasse　　E

SCIENTIFIC NAME: *Labroides phthirophagus*
AVERAGE SIZE: 2 - 3 inches
DESCRIPTION AND DISTINCTIVE FEATURES:
Bright yellow head and front of body with
broad line through eye. Tail and back of
body have distinct purplish-blue markings.
Juveniles lack yellow color.

DIET: Parasites and mucous off other fishes.
WHERE TO FIND THEM: On the reef at almost all depths within the recreational dive
limit. Endemic to Hawaii.
OBSERVATIONS: This species establishes cleaning stations on the reef and attracts fish
and eels by making distinct dart-like movements to advertise its services. While cleaning its host, it feeds on the host's excess mucous and parasites, setting a classic example of a mutually beneficial symbiotic relationship. Generally easy to approach.

COMMON NAME: Flame Wrasse　　E

SCIENTIFIC NAME: *Cirrhilabrus jordani*

AVERAGE SIZE: 3 - 4 inches
DESCRIPTION AND DISTINCTIVE FEATURES:
Males have bright red upper body, dorsal fin
and tail shading to whitish yellow on lower
body. Face has distinct yellow and red mark-
ings. Females are less brightly colored.
DIET: Zooplankton.
WHERE TO FIND THEM: At depths below 70
feet in areas with rubble a bottom. Endemic to Hawaii.
OBSERVATIONS: A fast-swimming species that is usually difficult to approach.

COMMON NAME: Smalltail Wrasse

SCIENTIFIC NAME: *Pseudojuloides cerasinus*

Male

AVERAGE SIZE: 3 - 4 inches
DESCRIPTION AND DISTINCTIVE FEATURES: Males
have a greenish body with a blue and yellow stripe
along body and a blue stripe on the side of head.
Females are mostly red with a yellow chest area.
DIET: Mollusks.
WHERE TO FIND THEM:
In rubble or reef areas usually below 60 feet.
OBSERVATIONS: Due to its habit of staying close to the
bottom, smaller size and initial shyness, this species is
often overlooked. If you remain in one place looking
for this fish, it often becomes curious and may
approach you.

Female

51

COMMON NAME: Shortnose Wrasse   E

SCIENTIFIC NAME: *Macropharyngodon geoffroy*
AVERAGE SIZE: 4 - 6 inches
DESCRIPTION AND DISTINCTIVE FEATURES:
Rows of blue spots on orange body,
blue lines on orange head.
DIET: Mollusks.
WHERE TO FIND THEM: Commonly seen
near outer reefs in areas with sand and   rub-
ble at depths from 20 to 100 feet,
feeding with other wrasses.
Endemic to Hawaii.
OBSERVATIONS: An active swimmer
which is difficult to get close to.

Female

Male

COMMON NAME: Hawaiian Hogfish

SCIENTIFIC NAME: *Bodianus bilunulatus*
HAWAIIAN NAME: A'awa
AVERAGE SIZE: 15 - 20 inches
DESCRIPTION AND DISTINCTIVE FEATURES: Bluish-
black spot on body near tail, yellow dorsal and anal
fin and tail. Brown lines through eye on upper
head. Red stripes along sides of body.

Juvenile

Adult

DIET: Small invertebrates.
WHERE TO FIND THEM: On seaward reefs
between 25 and 100 feet, near rubbly areas
foraging for food.
OBSERVATIONS: The hogfish can often be
observed following divers, hoping they dis-
rupt the bottom, which facilitates their food
search.

COMMON NAME: Hawaiian Knifefish   E

SCIENTIFIC NAME: *Cymolutes lecluse*

AVERAGE SIZE: 5 inches
DESCRIPTION AND DISTINCTIVE FEATURES:
Upper body gray, lower body white. Female
has small black spot at base of tail.
DIET: Small invertebrates buried in sand.
WHERE TO FIND THEM: In large sandy areas,
often quite a distance from the reef, to depths
below 50 feet. Endemic to Hawaii.

OBSERVATIONS: The careful, unobtrusive diver may be able to approach closely, but
if danger is suspected the knifefish will dive into the sand for protection.

COMMON NAME: Pavo Razor Wrasse

SCIENTIFIC NAME: *Xyrichtys pavo*

Juvenile

HAWAIIAN NAME: Laenihi
AVERAGE SIZE: 10 - 12 inches
DESCRIPTION AND DISTINCTIVE FEATURES: Juveniles have elongated dorsal spine, giving them an odd appearance. Adults have dark blotch on otherwise whitish-grey body.
DIET: Crabs and other small invertebrates buried in sand.
WHERE TO FIND THEM: In large sandy areas, often away from the reef in depths below 30 feet.
OBSERVATIONS: The careful, quiet diver may often approach closely, but if alarmed the razor wrasse will dive into the sand. If that happens, and you are patient, you can wait for them to emerge again a few minutes later.

COMMON NAME: Whitepatch Razor Wrasse

SCIENTIFIC NAME: *Xyrichtys aneitensis*
HAWAIIAN NAME: Laenihi
AVERAGE SIZE: 6 inches
DESCRIPTION AND DISTINCTIVE FEATURES: Cream color body with large white patch in center of body. Males have small yellow patch in front of white patch. Three faint dusky bars on body, more pronounced on upper part of body.
DIET: Crabs and small invertebrates buried in sand.

WHERE TO FIND THEM: In large sandy areas, often away from the reef in depths below 50 feet.
OBSERVATIONS: The careful, quiet diver may often approach closely, but if alarmed the razor wrasse will dive into the sand. If that happens, and you are patient, you can wait for them to emerge again a few minutes later.

SWIMS WITH PECTORAL FINS

53

Family: Parrotfishes - *Scaridae*

Parrotfishes derive their name from their fused teeth that resemble a parrot's beak. Among the largest and most colorful of Hawaii's reef fishes, parrotfishes are closely related to the wrasses and swim in a similar fashion. The predominant use of their pectoral fins for propulsion leaves their tail fin for an emergency burst of speed. Parrotfishes feed by scraping the algae from rocks and coral, as well as extracting algae living within the reef rock. A set of grinding plates located in the back of the fish's mouth grinds the reef rock until the final result is a fine sand that some tropical beaches are made of. One adult-sized parrotfish can make a ton of sand a year. On night encounters you can often observe parrotfishes sleeping inside a mucous cocoon which they secrete for protection from nocturnal predators. Female parrotfishes have the ability to change their sex and become supermales. More, these supermales are the largest and most colorful of all parrotfishes.

Photography: Like wrasses, most parrotfishes are difficult to get close to. To capture a daytime shot, you should sneak up on the parrotfish. If you see it disappear on one side of a coral head, swim around the other way and try to get your shot during that moment of surprise. Depending on the size of the parrotfish, a 60mm to 35mm lens works best. At night, when enveloped in its mucous cocoon, the parrotfish is easy prey for the photographer. You just can't place a framer on the cocoon, because as soon as you touch it, the parrotfish will bolt. Take the framer off and place the wand below the parrotfish, not touching the cocoon. For those of you utilizing a housed system, this is a great time for you to shoot a close-up of the eye or their beautiful pastel color patterns.

COMMON NAME: Bullethead Parrotfish
SCIENTIFIC NAME: *Chlororus sordidus*

A female Bullethead Parrotfish in its mucous cocoon at night.

HAWAIIAN NAME: Uhu
AVERAGE SIZE: 12 - 15 inches
DESCRIPTION AND DISTINCTIVE FEATURES:
Males overall pastel body, female brown-reddish with double row of white spots. White bar with a dark spot ahead of tail.
DIET: Algae and coral.

WHERE TO FIND THEM: On coral reefs at depths starting at 10 feet. Quite common.
OBSERVATIONS: Very skittish and difficult to get close to, except at night, when they are often found sleeping in a mucous cocoon and are easily observed and photographed.

COMMON NAME: Palenose Parrotfish

SCIENTIFIC NAME: *Scarus psittacus*

HAWAIIAN NAME: Uhu
AVERAGE SIZE: 6 - 11 inches
DESCRIPTION AND DISTINCTIVE FEATURES:
Pastel body, distinct blue lines on face and fins, yellow spot at base of tail. Females are dull brownish-grey.
DIET: Coral and algae.
WHERE TO FIND THEM: Very common in a variety of depths and habitats ranging from rich coral gardens to rubble areas.
OBSERVATIONS: Skittish when approached by divers, except at night, when they are often found sleeping in a mucous cocoon and are easily observed and photographed.

COMMON NAME: Stareye Parrotfish

SCIENTIFIC NAME: *Calotomus carolinus*

A female Stareye Parrotfish in its mucous cocoon at night.

HAWAIIAN NAME: Pōnuhunuhu
AVERAGE SIZE: 12 - 20 inches
DESCRIPTION AND DISTINCTIVE FEATURES:
Greenish-blue body with brown blotches. Pink lines radiating from eye giving it a star-like appearance. Female is reddish-brown. Note rough beak which differs from the smooth beak other parrotfishes have.

DIET: Leafy and encrusting algae.
WHERE TO FIND THEM: Found in a variety of depths and habitats ranging from rich coral gardens to rubble areas at depths below 10 feet.
OBSERVATIONS: Difficult to approach, except at night, when they are often found sleeping in a mucous cocoon and are easily observed and photographed.

A male Stareye Parrotfish in its mucous cocoon at night.

COMMON NAME: Redlip Parrotfish

SCIENTIFIC NAME: *Scarus rubroviolaceus*
HAWAIIAN NAME: Pālukaluka
AVERAGE SIZE: 20 - 25 inches
DESCRIPTION AND DISTINCTIVE FEATURES:
Male colorful, female with distinct bicolor
pattern, half light, half dark-reddish. Both
have square humped snout.

Female

Male

DIET: Algae and coral.
WHERE TO FIND THEM: Rocky and boulder areas, often in the surge zone, and shallow coral reefs.
OBSERVATIONS: One of the largest of the fish on the reef. Very skittish when approached by divers.

COMMON NAME: Spectacled Parrotfish   E

SCIENTIFIC NAME: *Chlorurus perspicillatus*

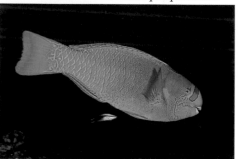

A male Spectacled Parrotfish at a cleaner station being cleaned by a Cleaner Wrasse.

HAWAIIAN NAME:
Uhu uliuli
AVERAGE SIZE:
16 - 22 inches
**DESCRIPTION AND
DISTINCTIVE FEATURES:** Body has
blue-greenish pattern with purple
overlay in males. Face has a blue-
edged purplish bar across forehead.
Females are reddish brown with a
light band ahead of the tail.
DIET: Algae and coral.

WHERE TO FIND THEM: Boulder and reef areas in shallow water. Not as common as
other parrotfishes. Endemic to Hawaii.
OBSERVATIONS: Very skittish when approached by divers.

SWIMS WITH PECTORAL FINS

Swims with Dorsal Fin

Triggerfishes - Filefishes

Swims with Dorsal Fin

Triggerfishes - Filefishes

Family: Triggerfishes - *Balistidae*

Triggerfishes are very territorial and aggressive toward other fishes and can even become aggressive toward humans when nesting. Some species have powerful jaws that allow them to feed on sea urchins and crustaceans, while others are plankton eaters. The triggerfish gets its family name from the two interlocking dorsal spines located to the rear of the eyes. When threatened, the triggerfish will retreat to a near-by hole and raise the first spine and lock it with the second spine, thus making it very difficult to remove the fish from its hiding place. Utilizing both their dorsal and anal fins, triggerfishes are very controlled swimmers and can move both forward and backward. They feed during the day and rest in holes at night.

Photography: Photography requires a housed system. Best shot with a 105mm due to shyness of most of these species.

COMMON NAME: Black Triggerfish

SCIENTIFIC NAME: *Melichthys niger*

HAWAIIAN NAME: Humuhumu ʻeleʻele
AVERAGE SIZE: 8 - 12 inches
DISTINCTIVE FEATURES: Normally black body with fine white line at base of dorsal fin and anal fin. Sometimes display color pattern featuring blue and yellow lines over part of body or whole body.
DIET: Algae and zooplankton.
WHERE TO FIND THEM: At various depths hovering over the reef in the water column.

OBSERVATIONS: Often seen in small aggregations. Naturally tend to be shy, and scurry into a protective crevice in the reef when approached by divers. In areas where fish are fed by humans, they lose all shyness and readily approach snorkelers and divers, while chasing more timid fish off the reef.

COMMON NAME: Pinktail Triggerfish

SCIENTIFIC NAME: *Melichthys vidua*
HAWAIIAN NAME: Humuhumu hiʻukole

AVERAGE SIZE: 10 - 12 inches
DISTINCTIVE FEATURES: Similar to black trigger, but has transparent dorsal and anal fin edged with black and a pink and white tail.
DIET: Algae, detritus, crabs, shrimps, small fishes and octopus.
WHERE TO FIND THEM: On seaward reefs at depths of at least 15 feet.

OBSERVATIONS: Naturally tend to be shy, and scurry into a protective crevice in the reef, when approached by divers.

COMMON NAME: Lagoon Triggerfish

SCIENTIFIC NAME: *Rhinecanthus aculeatus*
HAWAIIAN NAME: Humuhumu nukunuku apuaʻa

AVERAGE SIZE: 8 - 10 inches
DISTINCTIVE FEATURES: A very attractive color pattern consisting of yellow lips and yellow stripe along side of head. Blue bar along lips, blue lines over eye and along side of belly. Distinct white bands at rear of body.
DIET: Algae and invertebrates including mollusks, worms and crustaceans.
WHERE TO FIND THEM: In shallow bays and reefs on rubble and sandy areas. Seldom occurs deeper than 25 feet.

OBSERVATIONS: A very territorial fish that can get quite aggressive when protecting its eggs.

COMMON NAME: Picasso Triggerfish (Hawaii State Fish)

SCIENTIFIC NAME: *Rhinecanthus rectangulus*
HAWAIIAN NAME: Humuhumu nukunuku apuaʻa
AVERAGE SIZE: 7 - 9 inches
DISTINCTIVE FEATURES: A very attractive color pattern including blue lips, red spot at base of pectoral fins, golden triangle shaped lines at rear of body.
DIET: Algae and invertebrates including mollusks, worms and crustaceans.

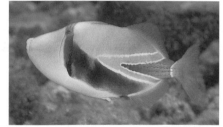

WHERE TO FIND THEM: Common on shallow reefs exposed to surge. Seldom occurs deeper than 25 feet.
OBSERVATIONS: A very skittish fish that is difficult to approach.

COMMON NAME: Lei or Whiteline Triggerfish

SCIENTIFIC NAME: *Sufflamen bursa*

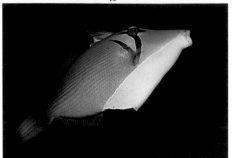

HAWAIIAN NAME: Humuhumu lei
AVERAGE SIZE: 6 - 7 inches
DISTINCTIVE FEATURES: White stripe from mouth to base of anal fin. Double bar (color may range from black to yellow) from pectoral fin over eye to base of pectoral fin. Body grey.
DIET: Algae and invertebrates including urchins, crustaceans and fish eggs.
WHERE TO FIND THEM: Below the surge zone on shallow reefs and in deeper areas with rock and rubble to 60 feet.
OBSERVATIONS: A very common and territorial fish that often attempts to charge divers. This fish is easily approached and photographed.

COMMON NAME: Bridled Triggerfish

SCIENTIFIC NAME: *Sufflamen fraenatus*

Female

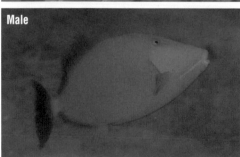

Male

HAWAIIAN NAME: Humuhumu mimi
AVERAGE SIZE: 10 - 12 inches
DISTINCTIVE FEATURES:
Males have a yellowish-white line running down from the corner of their mouth, reminding one of a bridle. Both males and females may have a white band around the base of their tail but are otherwise drab in color.
DIET: Invertebrates such as worms, sponges, crustaceans, brittle stars, urchins, and mollusks.
WHERE TO FIND THEM: Often near dropoffs and rubble areas in depths below 60 feet.
OBSERVATIONS:
This triggerfish is less common than other species and quite difficult to approach.

COMMON NAME: Bluegill Triggerfish

SCIENTIFIC NAME: *Xanthichthys auromarginatus*

Female

AVERAGE SIZE: 6 - 7 inches

DISTINCTIVE FEATURES: The males are the more colorful, with a bright blue chin and yellow lines on edges of dorsal and anal fin and tail. Otherwise grey body with white speckles. Females are recognized by blue ring around eye and blue tail.

DIET: Zooplankton

WHERE TO FIND THEM: Most commonly seen in depths below 50 feet hovering above the reef feeding on plankton.

Male

OBSERVATIONS: Often occur in small aggregations. This is a wary species which is quite difficult to get close to.

Family: Filefishes - *Monacanthidae*

Filefishes are closely related to triggerfishes, but the locking dorsal spines are located directly above the eyes, and they tend to be very shy. Filefishes are weak swimmers that have the ability to change color patterns to match their surroundings. During reproduction most species lay eggs which one of the parents guards. Like triggerfishes, filefishes move mostly by utilizing their dorsal and anal fins. Filefishes range from only a couple of inches to large species that may reach over 25 inches in length.

Photography: Most filefishes are shy and difficult to photograph, excluding the Barred Filefish, which readily approaches divers. The smaller species are best photographed with a 105mm macro lens, while the large Broomtail Filefish is best captured with a 28mm or 35mm lens.

COMMON NAME: Lacefin or Yellowtail Filefish

SCIENTIFIC NAME: *Pervagor aspricaudus*

HAWAIIAN NAME: 'O'ili
AVERAGE SIZE: 3 - 4 inches
DESCRIPTION AND DISTINCTIVE FEATURES:
Dark body, distinct yellow to orange tail.
DIET: Algae, sponges, tiny invertebrates.
WHERE TO FIND THEM: In rich coral areas at depths from 10 to 100 feet.
OBSERVATIONS: Very shy and skittish. Always remains within shelter of coral branches or reef crevices.

COMMON NAME: Fantail Filefish   E

SCIENTIFIC NAME: *Pervagor spilosoma*

HAWAIIAN NAME: 'O'ili uwi'uwi
AVERAGE SIZE: 4 - 5 inches
DESCRIPTION AND DISTINCTIVE FEATURES:
Interesting colorful pattern including black spots on whitish or golden body, brown lines on face. Bright orange, fan-like tail.
DIET: Algae, sponges, tiny invertebrates.
WHERE TO FIND THEM: On reefs at depths from 10 to 100 feet. Endemic to Hawaii.
OBSERVATIONS: Somewhat shy and skittish. Abundance has varied over the years. This species experiences a huge "population explosion" cycle, becoming the most common fish on the reef. It is said to occur approximately every forty years. This is followed by a massive die-off. The phenomenon was last recorded between 1985 and 1986.

COMMON NAME: Broomtail, Scribbled, or Scrolled Filefish

SCIENTIFIC NAME: *Aluterus scriptus*

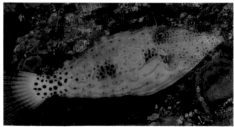

HAWAIIAN NAME: Loulu
AVERAGE SIZE: 20 - 25 inches
DESCRIPTION AND DISTINCTIVE FEATURES: Grey body with pastel blue lines and black spots. Fan-like tail.
DIET: Algae, sponges, hydrozoans.
WHERE TO FIND THEM: Found at a great variety of habitats and depths,

often seen on the reef, periodically in large schools.

OBSERVATIONS: One of the largest fish on Hawaiian reefs. Generally shy upon divers' and snorkelers' approach.

COMMON NAME: Barred Filefish

SCIENTIFIC NAME: *Cantherhines dumerilii*

HAWAIIAN NAME: 'O'ili

AVERAGE SIZE: 10 - 12 inches

DESCRIPTION AND DISTINCTIVE FEATURES: Body color ranges from grey to brown. White lips. Dark bars on side of body more or less visible.

DIET: Branching coral, urchins, sponges, mollusks and algae.

WHERE TO FIND THEM: This is a common fish on virtually all coral reefs at depths ranging from 10 to below 100 feet.

OBSERVATIONS: Can often be observed swimming in an odd sideways position. Reaction to divers ranges from shy to bold.

COMMON NAME: Hawaiian Filefish   E

SCIENTIFIC NAME: *Cantherhines sandwichiensis*

HAWAIIAN NAME: 'O'ili lepa

AVERAGE SIZE: 4 - 6 inches

DESCRIPTION AND DISTINCTIVE FEATURES: White spot at base of tail. Body color may range from whitish gray to brown. Fins sometimes yellow.

DIET: Mostly algae, but also coral, sponges and benthic animals.

WHERE TO FIND THEM: On the coral reef at a variety of depths. Endemic to Hawaii.

OBSERVATIONS: Usually shy upon approach.

COMMON NAME: Shy Filefish   E

SCIENTIFIC NAME: *Cantherhines verecundus*

HAWAIIAN NAME: 'O'ili
AVERAGE SIZE: 4 - 6 inches
DESCRIPTION AND DISTINCTIVE FEATURES: Dull grey body color with some mottling. Yellow eye.
DIET: Algae, sponges, small invertebrates.
WHERE TO FIND THEM: Always stays close to shelter near cracks and crevices of the reef. This uncommon species is endemic to Hawaii.
OBSERVATIONS: Very skittish upon divers approach.

SWIMS WITH DORSAL FIN

CHAPTER FIVE

Reddish, Bigeyes

Soldierfishes, Squirrelfishes, Bigeyes, Cardinalfishes

Reddish, Bigeyes

Soldierfishes, Squirrelfishes, Bigeyes, Cardinalfishes

Family: Soldierfishes and Squirrelfishes - *Holocentridae*

Soldierfishes and Squirrelfishes both belong to the same family. They are nocturnal and mostly reddish in color with large eyes. During the day they hide in caves and under ledges and seldom emerge onto the reef. Squirrelfishes have venomous spines near their cheeks, while soldierfishes tend to have a short, blunt snout.

Photography: Members of this nocturnal family are best photographed at night when they are out in the open, but can also be captured during the day if you make the effort to venture into caves. When photographing under ledges, be sure to adjust your strobes to aim them at the colorful fish, not the rocky ledge above. The best lens choice in most cases is the 60mm lens.

COMMON NAME: Bigscale Soldierfish
SCIENTIFIC NAME: *Myripristis berndti*

HAWAIIAN NAME: 'U'u
AVERAGE SIZE: 9 - 11 inches
DESCRIPTION AND DISTINCTIVE FEATURES: Dark bar at gill opening, otherwise red body. Note white lines at edge of fins, including tail.
DIET: Small crustaceans and large zooplankton.
WHERE TO FIND THEM: During the day, look under ledges and in caves for schooling Bigscale Soldierfish at depths below 30 feet. At night, found out in the open, searching for food.
OBSERVATIONS: A common species, which is very similar to the Brick Soldierfish, which lacks white edges on its fins.

COMMON NAME: Shoulderbar or Pearly Soldierfish

SCIENTIFIC NAME: *Myripristis kuntee*
HAWAIIAN NAME: ʻUʻu
AVERAGE SIZE: 5 - 7 inches
DESCRIPTION AND DISTINCTIVE FEATURES: Dark bar at gill opening. Body color may vary from pinkish-silver to orange-red. Tips of dorsal and anal fin and tail are usually of a more pronounced red edged with white.

DIET: Small crustaceans and large zooplankton.
WHERE TO FIND THEM: During the day the may be seen schooling on the open reef. At night they are generally found singularly searching for food at depths below ten feet.

COMMON NAME: Hawaiian Squirrelfish　　　E

SCIENTIFIC NAME: *Sargocentron xantherythrum*

HAWAIIAN NAME: ʻAlaʻihi
AVERAGE SIZE: 5 - 7 inches
DESCRIPTION AND DISTINCTIVE FEATURES: Red with silver stripes. Dorsal fin entirely red except for white tips.
DIET: Small crustaceans.
WHERE TO FIND THEM: During the day found in schools under ledges or in caves. At night look for them on the open reef actively feeding. Endemic to Hawaii.
OBSERVATIONS: A common species that is relatively easy to approach.

COMMON NAME: Long-jawed or Saber Squirrelfish

SCIENTIFIC NAME: *Sargocentron spiniferum*

HAWAIIAN NAME: ʻAlaʻihi mama
AVERAGE SIZE: 12 - 14 inches
DESCRIPTION AND DISTINCTIVE FEATURES: Solid red body, but all fins, except dorsal have yellow markings. Has large venomous spine at gill cover.
DIET: Small crustaceans and small fishes.
WHERE TO FIND THEM: During the day, look under ledges, in caves and caverns, and among boulders at depths as shallow as 10 feet, down to below 100 feet. At night they can be found on the open reef.
OBSERVATIONS: This is the largest squirrelfish in Hawaii.

COMMON NAME: Tahitian Squirrelfish

SCIENTIFIC NAME: *Sargocentron tiere*
HAWAIIAN NAME: 'Ala'ihi
AVERAGE SIZE: 12 - 14 inches
DESCRIPTION AND DISTINCTIVE
FEATURES: Crimson red body
has iridescent blue lines along
side of body and on edges of
pelvic and anal fins.
DIET: Small crustaceans.

WHERE TO FIND THEM: During the day, look under ledges, in caves and caverns, and among boulders at depths as shallow as 10 feet, down to below 100 feet. At night they can be found on the open reef.
OBSERVATIONS: An uncommon species in Hawaii.

COMMON NAME: Spotfin Squirrelfish

SCIENTIFIC NAME: *Neoniphon sammara*
HAWAIIAN NAME: 'Ala'ihi
AVERAGE SIZE: 8 - 10 inches
DESCRIPTION AND DISTINCTIVE
FEATURES: Silver body with red-
dish-brown horizontal lines.
Dark spot on dorsal fin.
DIET: Small crustaceans.
WHERE TO FIND THEM: Can be

seen during the day on the reef, inside or staying close to a crevice or ledge. At night they are found out in the open to feed.
OBSERVATIONS: This species is generally quite approachable.

Family: Bigeyes - *Priacanthidae*

Often confused with squirrelfishes or soldierfishes because of similar habits and coloration, Bigeyes are not related and have different body shapes. Most often they are observed with a red body coloration, but are able to assume a silvery color in a matter of seconds.

Photography: Bigeyes tend to hover stationary and are quite easily photographed with practically every lens, in either a housing or on a Nikonos camera without macro framer.

COMMON NAME: Glasseye

SCIENTIFIC NAME: *Heteropriacanthus cruentatus*

HAWAIIAN NAME: 'Āweoweo
AVERAGE SIZE: 10 - 12 inches
DESCRIPTION AND DISTINCTIVE FEATURES: Although the glasseye may appear solid red, it is usually recognized by the silvery blotches all over its body, and round spots on the tail.
DIET: Zooplankton.

WHERE TO FIND THEM: During the day in caves and underneath ledges at depths below twenty feet. At night they can be observed above the reef, feeding in the water column.

OBSERVATIONS: Once spotted, glass eyes are generally quite approachable.

COMMON NAME: Hawaiian Bigeye   E

SCIENTIFIC NAME: *Priacanthus meeki*
HAWAIIAN NAME: 'Āweoweo
AVERAGE SIZE: 10 - 12 inches
DESCRIPTION AND DISTINCTIVE FEATURES: Although capable of changing to silver, the endemic Hawaiian Bigeye is most often seen in a solid red color with dark blotches along the lateral line.

DIET: Zooplankton.

WHERE TO FIND THEM: During the day in caves and underneath ledges at depths below twenty feet. At night time they can be observed above the reef, feeding in the water column. Endemic to Hawaii.

OBSERVATIONS: Once spotted, Bigeyes are generally quite approachable, sometimes even approaching divers curiously. Tends to hover motionless in dark holes while Squirrelfishes nervously dart about when approached.

Family: Cardinal fishes - *Apogonidae*

More colorful in the Indo-Pacific, in Hawaii these small nocturnal fishes are quite drab in color. In most species, the male broods the eggs in his mouth until they hatch. Due to less eye-catching color patterns, small size, and secretive daytime habits, this family is commonly overlooked.

Photography: Because of their less-attractive color pattern, these fishes make less popular photo subjects, although they are very easily photographed.

COMMON NAME: Oddscale Cardinalfish

SCIENTIFIC NAME: *Apogon evermanni*

HAWAIIAN NAME: 'Upāpalu
AVERAGE SIZE: 4 - 5 inches
DESCRIPTION AND DISTINCTIVE FEATURES: Dark stripe through eye, white spot behind second dorsal fin.
DIET: Zooplankton and small crustaceans.
WHERE TO FIND THEM: In recesses of caves and lava formations, usually at 40 feet and deeper.
OBSERVATIONS: Best observed with flashlight, since these fish rarely emerge into the open.

REDDISH, BIGEYES

COMMON NAME: Iridescent Cardinalfish

SCIENTIFIC NAME: *Apogon kallopterus*

HAWAIIAN NAME: 'Upāpalu
AVERAGE SIZE: 4 - 5 inches
DESCRIPTION AND DISTINCTIVE FEATURES: Black stripe from snout through eye along side of body. Black spot at base of tail.
DIET: Zooplankton and small crustaceans.
WHERE TO FIND THEM: On shallow reefs, including turbid areas. Common on sandy reefs at night.
OBSERVATIONS: Best observed with flashlight, since these fish remain beneath ledges during the day. At night they emerge and a blue-green iridescence is visible.

COMMON NAME: Bandfin Cardinalfish

SCIENTIFIC NAME: *Apogon taeniopterus*
HAWAIIAN NAME: 'Upāpalu

AVERAGE SIZE: 5 - 6 inches
DESCRIPTION AND DISTINCTIVE FEATURES: Black and white markings on all fins including tail.
DIET: Zooplankton and small crustaceans.
WHERE TO FIND THEM: Hides underneath ledges and crevices during the day but can be seen out in the open at night. Prefers hard reefs with good coral growth.
OBSERVATIONS: Best observed with flashlight, since these fish remain beneath ledges during the day.

CHAPTER SIX

Heavy Body, Large Lips

Groupers - Basslets (Anthias)

Heavy Body, Large Lips

Groupers - Basslets (Anthias)

Family: Groupers and Basslets - *Serranidae*

Large groupers are often referred to as sea basses, while the small and delicate anthias is known as a basslet. The most common grouper in Hawaii, the Peacock Grouper, is very shy and difficult to approach. Groupers and anthias commonly go through sex reversal. They all begin life as females and change into males. Most anthias remain female, living in harems that are dominated by one male.

Photography: The species of basslets we have in Hawaii are really quite easy to photograph once you locate them. Unfortunately it is often deep. Hawaiian basslets don't dart around as much as their counterparts from other parts of the Indo- Pacific. For a full-frame shot, you will need a housed camera utilizing either a 60mm or 105mm lens. Your approach should be slow and non-threatening. Peacock groupers are best captured with a wide angle lens, such as a 28mm or 35mm lens. This is usually a difficult fish to approach. You will need to sneak up on them, since they usually take off as soon as a diver approaches. This is especially the case in areas which spearfishermen frequent.

COMMON NAME: Peacock Grouper

SCIENTIFIC NAME: *Cephalopholis argus*
HAWAIIAN NAME: Roi
AVERAGE SIZE: 12 - 15 inches
DESCRIPTION AND DISTINCTIVE FEATURES: Iridescent blue spots on entire body, including fins and tail. Five light bars on rear part of body which may not always be visible.
DIET: Fishes and crustaceans.
WHERE TO FIND THEM: Below 20 feet on exposed reefs and in protected bays, usually resting on a coral head.
OBSERVATIONS: This species was introduced from French Polynesia in 1956 as a food source. Upon divers' approach, this fish usually responds skittish, diving into shelter.

COMMON NAME: Bicolor Anthias

SCIENTIFIC NAME: *Pseudanthias bicolor*

AVERAGE SIZE:
4 - 5 inches

**DESCRIPTION
AND DISTINCTIVE
FEATURES:**
Upper body orange,
lower half pink. Note
two elongated dorsal
spines with bright
yellow tip.

DIET: Zooplankton.

WHERE TO FIND

This Bicolor Anthias is photographed while in the feeding process.

THEM: At depths below 70 feet on prominent outcrops in otherwise sandy, current-swept areas.

OBSERVATIONS: Bicolor Anthias are easily approached by divers.

COMMON NAME: Longfin Anthias   E

SCIENTIFIC NAME: *Pseudanthias hawaiiensis*

AVERAGE SIZE:
2 - 4 inches

**DESCRIPTION AND
DISTINCTIVE FEATURES:**
Stunning color patterns
including orange, yellow,
and on males, pink on the
base of tail. Irregular pink-
ish markings on face. Long
pelvic fins.

DIET: Zooplankton.

WHERE TO FIND THEM: At
depths below 100 feet on
reefs or boulder areas. This
relative of *Pseudanthias
ventralis* is endemic to
Hawaii.

OBSERVATIONS: When
carefully approached, the
Longfin Anthias often
responds with curiosity.

COMMON NAME: Yellow Anthias E

SCIENTIFIC NAME: *Holanthias fuscipinnis*

© MIKE SEVERNS

AVERAGE SIZE:
6 - 7 inches

DESCRIPTION AND DISTINCTIVE FEATURES:
Yellow body with magenta lines.

DIET: Zooplankton and small invertebrates.

WHERE TO FIND THEM:
Normally occurs at depths below 180 feet but occasionally seen at 140 feet. Endemic to Hawaii.

OBSERVATIONS: If you spot one of these beautiful anthias, check your dive computer and depth gauge!

HEAVY BODY, LARGE LIPS

CHAPTER SEVEN

Oddshaped Swimmers

Puffers - Spiny Puffer - Trunkfishes - Goatfishes

ODDSHAPED SWIMMERS

Oddshaped Swimmers

Puffers - Spiny Puffer - Trunkfishes - Goatfishes

Family: Puffers - *Tetraodontidae*
and Spiny Puffer - *Diodontidae*

Puffers are slow-swimming fishes that have the unique ability to draw water into a specialized chamber to inflate their bodies. This inflation is their primary defense against predators. If threatened, they will often swim into a hole and inflate themselves, making it impossible to get them out. Though it was popular to catch a puffer and watch it inflate, it is traumatic to the animal and should be avoided. Puffer is a culinary delicacy in Japan, but must be prepared properly or it can be deadly. Nevertheless, eating this extremely toxic fish is considered risky.

Photography: Puffers are fairly slow-moving creatures, and can be photographed with a variety of lenses and framers, depending on the size and nature of the individual.

COMMON NAME: Porcupine Puffer

SCIENTIFIC NAME: *Diodon hystrix*
HAWAIIAN NAME: Kokala

AVERAGE SIZE: 22 - 25 inches
DESCRIPTION AND DISTINCTIVE FEATURES: Black spots and spines all over body and fins. Large eyes and head.
DIET: Crabs and other invertebrates.
WHERE TO FIND THEM: Generally hiding under ledges and in caves during the day, but in some areas, such as Kealakekua Bay, they are frequently observed hovering high in the water column above the reef.
OBSERVATIONS: This is the largest of the puffers. When threatened, they puff up and display their spines for defense.

COMMON NAME: Stripebelly Puffer

SCIENTIFIC NAME: *Arothron hispidus*
HAWAIIAN NAME: 'O'opu hue
AVERAGE SIZE: 14 - 18 inches

DESCRIPTION AND DISTINCTIVE FEATURES: White spots over olive green body. White belly.
DIET: A wide variety of invertebrates and algae.
WHERE TO FIND THEM: Habitats are as varied as the diet: Shallow bays to deep current-swept dropoffs.
OBSERVATIONS: Usually allows divers and snorkelers to approach within a few feet.

COMMON NAME: Spotted Puffer

SCIENTIFIC NAME: *Arothon meleagris*
HAWAIIAN NAME: 'O'opu hue
AVERAGE SIZE: 10 - 12 inches
DESCRIPTION AND DISTINCTIVE FEATURES: White spots all over brown body. A yellow phase is possible, but uncommon in Hawaii.
DIET: Coral (mostly), algae, sponges

and some mollusks.
WHERE TO FIND THEM: Singularly on the coral reef below 10 feet.
OBSERVATIONS: When threatened, this puffer often hides in a crevice on the reef, inflating and wedging itself in.

COMMON NAME: Hawaiian Whitespotted Toby   E

SCIENTIFIC NAME: *Canthigaster jactator*
AVERAGE SIZE: 2 - 3 inches

DESCRIPTION AND DISTINCTIVE FEATURES: Emerald green eyes, white spots on brown body.
DIET: Sponge, algae, and small invertebrates.
WHERE TO FIND THEM: Commonly found at various depths on reefs. Endemic to Hawaii.
OBSERVATIONS: A very bold, curious puffer, often seen in pairs. Easy to get close to.

ODDSHAPED SWIMMERS

COMMON NAME: Ambon Toby

SCIENTIFIC NAME: *Canthigaster amboinensis*
AVERAGE SIZE: 3 - 4 inches
DESCRIPTION AND DISTINCTIVE FEATURES:
Blue lines radiating from eye, blue spots over brown body, dark irregular lines on lower head.
DIET: Algae, detritus and invertebrates.
WHERE TO FIND THEM: In shallow boulder habitat in the surge zone, sometimes deeper coral reefs.

OBSERVATIONS: The Ambon Toby is cautious, but not too skittish when approached. They are surprisingly fast swimmers, and best observed from a short distance.

COMMON NAME: Crown Toby

SCIENTIFIC NAME: *Canthigaster coronata*
AVERAGE SIZE: 3 - 4 inches
DESCRIPTION AND DISTINCTIVE FEATURES:
Four dark saddles over body and head. Yellow speckles from snout to tail.
DIET: Algae, detritus, and small invertebrates.
WHERE TO FIND THEM: In rubble and boulder areas below 30 feet.
OBSERVATIONS: Usually observed in pairs. This species is easy to approach by the unobtrusive diver.

COMMON NAME: Lantern Toby

SCIENTIFIC NAME: *Canthigaster epilampra*

AVERAGE SIZE: 3 - 4 inches
DESCRIPTION AND DISTINCTIVE FEATURES: Upper body brown, lower body white. Iridescent blue and yellow lines radiate from eyes. Yellow tail. Note emerald green eyes.
DIET: Algae, detritus, invertebrates.
WHERE TO FIND THEM: Usually seen below 80 feet.
OBSERVATIONS: Often seen in pairs. The Lantern Toby is cautious, but not too skittish when approached.

Family: Trunkfishes - *Ostraciontidae*

Because of their similar shape, trunkfishes are often mistaken for puffers. However, trunkfishes are not able to inflate themselves and their body is actually a shell that has small gaps for its eyes, mouth, gill openings, anus, and caudal peduncle. Trunkfishes move slowly and are territorial by nature. They begin life as females from which some experience a sex change and turn into males. Females are sighted much more frequently than the more colorful males.

Photography: With a little bit of patience and a macro lens, it is usually quite easy to successfully photograph these wary but curious fish.

COMMON NAME: Spotted Trunkfish or Boxfish

SCIENTIFIC NAME: *Ostracion meleagis*
AVERAGE SIZE: 2 - 4 inches
DESCRIPTION AND DISTINCTIVE FEATURES:
Males bright blue, top of squarish body orange with white spots. Females uniformly brown with white spots.
DIET: Algae, sponges, encrusting invertebrates.

Female

Male

WHERE TO FIND THEM: Found most often hiding in crevices in the reef. Sometimes seen out in the open hovering close to shelter.
OBSERVATIONS: A wary species that retreats into shelter when approached, but often becomes curious after a moment and emerges again.

COMMON NAME: Whitley's Trunkfish

SCIENTIFIC NAME: *Ostracion whitleyi*
AVERAGE SIZE: 3 - 5 inches
DESCRIPTION AND DISTINCTIVE FEATURES:
Males blue, with two white lines at edges of side of body. White spots on top of body. Females brown with one broad wide band at side of body, white spots on top of body.
DIET: Algae, sponges, encrusting invertebrates.

Female

WHERE TO FIND THEM: Found most often hiding in crevices in the reef. Sometimes seen out in the open hovering close to shelter. Males very rare in Hawaii.
OBSERVATIONS: A little bit bolder than the Spotted Trunkfish. Can often be observed up close.

Family: Goatfishes - *Mullidae*

Goatfishes are easily recognized by the two retractable barbels under the chin which they use as delicate sensors to locate food. When feeding you will usually find this fish singularly. While resting, many species can be observed in stationary aggregations over sand patches. Many goatfishes have the ability to quickly and dramatically change colors, from a resting pattern to an active pattern. Some feed by day and night, while other species of goatfish feed only at night. All are common in Hawaii.

Photography: Goatfishes are easily photographed during day and night dives. Schooling goatfishes are best captured with any wide angle lens, while the 60mm macro lens is best for portrait shots. At night it may be possible to place a Nikonos close-up framer around the animal, or remove the framer and use the wand to   measure distance.

COMMON NAME: Blue Goatfish

SCIENTIFIC NAME: *Parupeneus cyclostomus*

HAWAIIAN NAME: Moano kea, Moano kali
AVERAGE SIZE: 15 - 18 inches
DESCRIPTION AND DISTINCTIVE FEATURES: Blue lines on head, dorsal fin and tail. Yellow blotch between dorsal fin and tail.
DIET: Small fishes and crustaceans.
WHERE TO FIND THEM: Found singularly or in small groups foraging actively on the reef. They can be found from the surge zone to below 100 feet. At night they are found sleeping in the open.

OBSERVATIONS: Daytime feeder. Sometimes responds skittish to approaching divers. It is very common to observe one or more Blue Goatfish foraging the reef accompanied by the Blue Trevally. Occasionally moray eels or octopus can be seen following this "gang". Juvenile goatfishes often follow wrasses in the same manner.

COMMON NAME: Double bar Goatfish

SCIENTIFIC NAME: *Parupeneus bifasciatus*

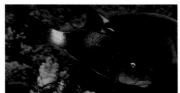

HAWAIIAN NAME: Munu
AVERAGE SIZE: 10 - 12 inches
DESCRIPTION AND DISTINCTIVE FEATURES: Color may vary, but two broad bars are faint to strongly visible. Caudal peduncle is always white.
DIET: Small crustaceans and fishes.

WHERE TO FIND THEM: Rocky/exposed reefs deeper than 20 feet.

OBSERVATIONS: This species forages for food by day and night. Usually seen solitary. Easily approached when resting on rock shelves. Less common than the Manybar Goatfish.

COMMON NAME: Manybar Goatfish

SCIENTIFIC NAME: *Parupeneus multifasciatus*

HAWAIIAN NAME: Moana, Moano
AVERAGE SIZE: 5 - 7 inches
DESCRIPTION AND DISTINCTIVE FEATURES:
Color may vary, but black bar behind eye, black bars at rear half of body always more or less visible.
DIET: Small crustaceans and invertebrates.

WHERE TO FIND THEM: A common fish which is observed feeding in sand and rubble areas near the reef.

OBSERVATIONS: This species feeds during the day and is inactive at night. Easily approached by divers and often curious.

COMMON NAME: Yellowfin Goatfish

SCIENTIFIC NAME: *Mulloidichthys vanicolensis*
HAWAIIAN NAME: Weke 'ula
AVERAGE SIZE: 10 - 14 inches
DESCRIPTION AND DISTINCTIVE FEATURES: Yellow stripe from eye to tail along side of body. Yellow tail and yellow fins. Iris of eye is red.
DIET: Small crustaceans and fishes.

WHERE TO FIND THEM: Often found in large schools over sandy patches below 20 feet during the day. At night they forage singularly in sand and rubble areas.

OBSERVATIONS: A nocturnal feeder that rests during the day. Easily approached especially while resting.

COMMON NAME: Yellowstripe Goatfish

SCIENTIFIC NAME: *Mulloidichthys flavolineatus*
HAWAIIAN NAME: Weke
AVERAGE SIZE: 10 - 16 inches
DESCRIPTION AND DISTINCTIVE FEATURES:
Similar to Yellowfin Goatfish, but this species has no yellow on fins and tail. The middle of the yellow stripe has a black spot which is usually visible.
DIET: Small crustaceans and invertebrates.

WHERE TO FIND THEM: Common over shallow sandy patches in large schools, but more frequently found in small groups or pairs. Feeding occurs during day and night.

OBSERVATIONS: Easily approached. It creates circular depressions while foraging for prey buried in the sand.

COMMON NAME: Whitesaddle Goatfish   E

SCIENTIFIC NAME: *Parupeneus porphyreus*
HAWAIIAN NAME: Kumu
AVERAGE SIZE: 12 - 14 inches
DESCRIPTION AND DISTINCTIVE FEATURES:
Color may vary from whitish-gray to purple or pink. White spot at base of second dorsal fin and a striped pattern through face and eye.

DIET: Small crustaceans and fishes.
WHERE TO FIND THEM: This species hides under boulders and ledges in small groups during the day, from 10 to below 100 feet. Endemic to Hawaii.
OBSERVATIONS: Feeds primarily at night singularly.

COMMON NAME: Bandtail Goatfish   E

SCIENTIFIC NAME: *Upeneus arge*

HAWAIIAN NAME: Weke pueo
AVERAGE SIZE: 10 - 12 inches
DESCRIPTION AND DISTINCTIVE FEATURES: Silvery body with brownish stripes on side of body. Distinctive pattern of black and white cross-bands on tail.

DIET: Small crustaceans and invertebrates.
WHERE TO FIND THEM: Seen in shallow water on sandy bottoms near reefs and in turbid bays.
OBSERVATIONS: Can be seen singularly or in small schools. Difficult to get close to.

COMMON NAME: Sidespot Goatfish

SCIENTIFIC NAME: *Parupeneus pleurostigma*

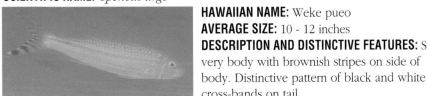

HAWAIIAN NAME: Malu
AVERAGE SIZE: 10 inches
DESCRIPTION AND DISTINCTIVE FEATURES:
Pinkish-white body with small iridescent blue spots on upper body. Large black spot on each side of body surrounded by light area.

DIET: Small crustaceans and invertebrates.
WHERE TO FIND THEM: Shallow sand and rubble areas above 130 feet near reefs.
OBSERVATIONS: Not as common as most other goatfishes in Hawaii. Does not allow divers to approach closely. Sleeps in sand pockets on the reef at night.

CHAPTER EIGHT

Elongated Body

Pipefish - Seahorse - Trumpetfish - Cornetfish - Tilefish

Elongated Body

Pipefish - Seahorse - Trumpetfish - Cornetfish - Tilefish

Family:
Pipefishes and Seahorses - *Syngnathidae*

Seahorses and pipefishes have long tubular snouts and a rigid body. During reproduction, the female deposits its eggs in the male's specialized pouch. The male then keeps and tends the eggs until hatching.

Photography: Pipefishes and seahorses are slow-moving creatures that can be photographed with a framer and macro or close-up kit, as well as any macro lens.

COMMON NAME: Redstriped Pipefish E

SCIENTIFIC NAME: *Dunckerocampus baldwini*

AVERAGE SIZE: 4 - 5 inches

DESCRIPTION AND DISTINCTIVE FEATURES: Elongated body, red stripe along head and body.

DIET: Tiny, free-swimming crustaceans (copepods).

WHERE TO FIND THEM: Under ledges and in caves, often near the ceiling or walls. Only found in Hawaii, as shallow as 20 feet, down to depths beyond the recreational dive limit.

OBSERVATIONS: Pipefish are difficult to find due to their size, cryptic habit and camouflaging abilities, but quite approachable once spotted. This pipefish can sometimes be observed cleaning other fishes.

COMMON NAME: Spotted Seahorse

SCIENTIFIC NAME: *Hippocampus kuda*

AVERAGE SIZE: 10 inches

DESCRIPTION AND DISTINCTIVE FEATURES: Its unique shape, and spines on head and body. Color may vary, from yellow, brown, reddish to black, and spots are not always visible.

DIET: Possibly zooplankton and free swimming, tiny crustaceans (copepods).

WHERE TO FIND THEM: Occasionally seen in protected, often turbid bays or drifting with clusters of seaweed or other flotsam in the open ocean at depths ranging from the surface down to depths below 100 feet.

OBSERVATIONS: Once found, the seahorse is easily approached. Tiny, newly hatched seahorses immediately ascend to the surface to swallow a tiny bit of air, which allows them to stay in their upright position.

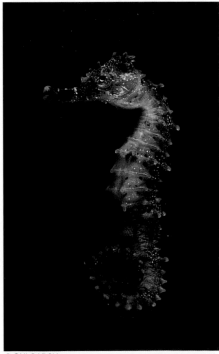

© GUI GARCIA

Family: Cornetfish - *Fistulariidae* and Trumpetfish - *Aulostomidae*

Cornetfish and trumpetfish are often confused because of their similar shape. One distinctive difference is the whip like tail versus the fan tail of the trumpetfish. Cornetfish often school with others of approximately the same size over sandy rubble areas. Trumpetfish are generally seen singularly. Both species are very aggressive ambush hunters, having the ability to change color and position themselves to blend into their surroundings. They use coral heads, sea urchins, and other natural objects to hide among, as well as man-made structures or divers' bodies.

Photography: Both Cornetfish and Trumpetfish often allow divers to approach closely and are easily photographed. Due to their length, they are best captured with a 35mm, 28mm or 20mm lens.

COMMON NAME: Trumpetfish

SCIENTIFIC NAME: *Aulostomus chinensis*

Brown Phase

HAWAIIAN NAME: Nūnū
AVERAGE SIZE: 20 - 30 inches
DESCRIPTION AND DISTINCTIVE FEATURES:
Occurs in various color phases. Body may be solid yellow or appear in a range of grayish-brown tones. During gray phase often confused with Cornetfish. The most distinctive difference is the Trumpetfish's fan-like tail.
WHERE TO FIND THEM: This is an ambush hunter which often uses schools of grazing surgeonfishes, or other herbivores for cover when hunting its prey. When prey is sighted, the Trumpetfish

Yellow Phase

suddenly darts out the school and sucks in the unsuspecting victim with a vacuum-like action. Trumpetfish change their color and position their bodies to blend into the background. When approached by divers they generally remain still to maintain their camouflage, but will move away if pursued.

COMMON NAME: Cornetfish

SCIENTIFIC NAME: *Fistularia commersonii*

HAWAIIAN NAME: Nūnū peke

AVERAGE SIZE: 2 - 4 feet

DESCRIPTION AND DISTINCTIVE FEATURES: Elongated silver body, whip-like tail. Sometimes flashes two rows of blue spots or lines.

DIET: Small fishes and crustaceans.

WHERE TO FIND THEM: Hovering above the reef or sand and rubble areas, from shallow reefs to generally at least 80 feet.

OBSERVATIONS: This is an ambush hunter which stalks its prey. Occasionally occurs in small groups of 4 - 6. Quite approachable and sometimes curious enough to approach a diver, especially when eye contact is avoided.

Family: Tilefish - *Malacanthidae*

These fish belong to a small family of elongated fishes which dwell in sandy or rubbly areas. Commonly they are seen hovering above the bottom. They move in a distinctive undulating pattern and do many quick starts and stops as they carefully watch for enemies or detect buried prey. Only one species occurs in Hawaii.

COMMON NAME: Flagtail Tilefish

SCIENTIFIC NAME: *Malacanthus brevirostris*

AVERAGE SIZE: 7 - 10 inches

DESCRIPTION AND DISTINCTIVE FEATURES: Two black stripes on tail, otherwise silvery-gray body with faint bands.

DIET: Buried invertebrates.

WHERE TO FIND THEM:

In sand and rubble areas at depths of at least 30 feet, more often at 60 - 70 feet.

OBSERVATIONS: Builds a burrow under a loose rock or rubble piece. It is generally observed hovering near the burrow's entrance, undulating its body. When divers attempt to approach closely it disappears into its burrow. For a close view, try to maneuver yourself between the fish and its burrow.

ELONGATED BODY

CHAPTER NINE

Small Bottom Dwellers

Blennies - Gobies - Dartfishes

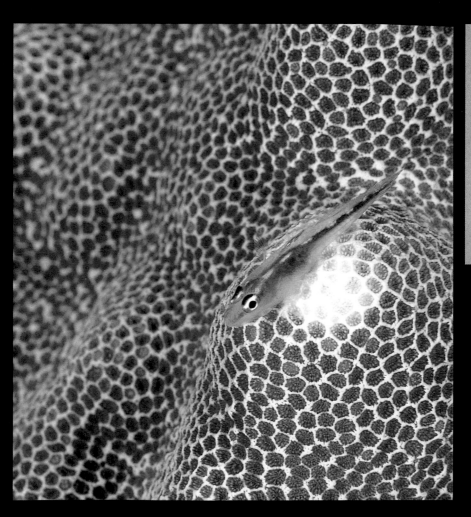

Small Bottom Dwellers

Blennies - Gobies - Dartfishes

Family: Blennies - *Blenniidae*

These small fishes are commonly overlooked by divers and snorkelers due to their size, camouflage, and skittish behavior. Most of them are bottom dwellers with no swim bladder, and are usually seen perched on a piece of coral or peering from holes. Sabertooth blennies possess a swim bladder and are commonly observed free-swimming.

Photography: Because of their "cute" faces with interesting eyelash-like filaments (cirri), blennies are favorite underwater photo subjects. Unfortunately, they are quite shy, and are best photographed from a distance. A housed camera is a must, utilizing a 105-200mm lens. Your approach should be very slow and non-threatening.

COMMON NAME: Scarface Blenny   E

SCIENTIFIC NAME: *Cirripectes vanderbilti*
HAWAIIAN NAME: Pao'o
AVERAGE SIZE: 3 inches
DESCRIPTION AND DISTINCTIVE FEATURES: Red ring around eye, red, irregular speckles and lines on its (cute) face. Cirri above eyes.
DIET: Benthic algae.
WHERE TO FIND THEM: Usually between 2 and 30 feet, perched on coral or rocks. Endemic to Hawaii.
OBSERVATIONS: Due to its small size and skittish behavior, this blenny is often

overlooked by snorkelers or divers. Best observed from a distance. Upon approach, the scarface blennies will dive into cover.

COMMON NAME: Leopard or Shortbodied Blenny

SCIENTIFIC NAME: *Exallias brevis*

Female

HAWAIIAN NAME: Pao'o kauila
AVERAGE SIZE: 4 - 6 inches
DESCRIPTION AND DISTINCTIVE FEATURES:
Leopard-like pattern all over head and body.

Male

Males have a red hue on body.

DIET: Coral polyps.
WHERE TO FIND THEM: On shallow reefs, usually tucked away in the protection of the coral.
OBSERVATIONS: Very skittish when approached by divers. Best observed from a distance.

COMMON NAME: Ewa Fangblenny or Sabertooth Blenny   E

SCIENTIFIC NAME: *Plagiotremus ewaensis*
AVERAGE SIZE: 3 inches
DESCRIPTION AND DISTINCTIVE FEATURES: Two vivid blue stripes along sides of body from snout to tail.
DIET: Mucus, scales, and skin of other fishes.
WHERE TO FIND THEM: Below a depth of 20 feet hovering above the reef or tucked away in its home, which consists of abandoned worm tubes.

Watch for the blenny's tiny head poking out of the hole, surveying the territory for its next victim. Endemic to Hawaii.

OBSERVATIONS: This blenny has been nicknamed the "imposter," due to its dangerous and challenging lifestyle. Sabertooth blennies sneak attack larger fish, taking a bite out of them. Often they mimic a cleaner wrasse. When the host fish responds, the blenny bites a scale or chunk of flesh out of the unsuspecting victim. A solitary species, unlike Gosline's Fangblenny.

COMMON NAME: Gosline's Fangblenny or Sabertooth Fangblenny   E

SCIENTIFIC NAME: *Plagiostremus goslinei*
AVERAGE SIZE: 2 inches
DESCRIPTION AND DISTINCTIVE FEATURES: Lower body white, upper body brownish-yellow with a narrow light line along top part of body.
DIET: Mucus, scales, and skin of other fishes.
WHERE TO FIND THEM: Below a depth of 20 feet, hovering above the reef or tucked away in its

home, which consists of abandoned worm tubes. Watch for the blenny's tiny head poking out of the hole, surveying the territory for its next victim. Endemic to Hawaii.

OBSERVATIONS: Sabertooth blennies sneak attack larger fish, taking a bite out of them. Often, they mimic a cleaner wrasse, and when the host fish responds the blenny bites a scale or piece of flesh out of the unsuspecting victim. Several blennies may be seen together in the open.

Family: Gobies - *Gobiidae*
and Dartfishes - *Microdesmidae*

Though one of the largest fish families, gobies are commonly overlooked by snorkelers and divers due to their tiny size. The pelvic fins of many goby species are fused together and have developed into a suction cup, which enables them to cling to objects. Most are bottom dwellers that lack a swim bladder, while some species, such as the dartfish, are able to hover above the bottom. When reproducing, gobies lay an egg mass, which is then guarded by the male.

Photography: All gobies are easily photographed with a 60mm or 105mm macro lens. Images of the gorgonian goby and the wire coral goby can also be captured using a framer with a macro kit.

COMMON NAME: Eye-bar Goby

SCIENTIFIC NAME: *Gnatholepsis anjerensis*
AVERAGE SIZE: 2 - 3 inches

DESCRIPTION AND DISTINCTIVE FEATURES: Color pattern may very from dark spots, to blotches and lines on grayish body. Note small yellow spot above pectoral fin. Emerald green eyes with a thin dark bar below.
DIET: Small fishes and crustaceans.

WHERE TO FIND THEM: In sandy or rubble areas near reefs, often in bays with limited visibility. Due to their excellent camouflage you'll need to slow down and observe sand and rubble areas closely.

OBSERVATIONS: This small fish relies on its camouflage for defense and is quite approachable once spotted.

COMMON NAME: Hawaiian Sand Goby

SCIENTIFIC NAME: *Coryphopterus sp.*

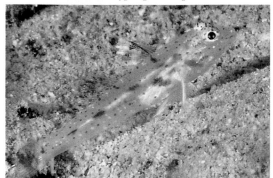

AVERAGE SIZE: 1 1/2 inches
DESCRIPTION AND DISTINCTIVE FEATURES: Translucent body with dark brown and orange speckles and blotches. Black spot at base of tail.
DIET: Small crustaceans and invertebrates.
WHERE TO FIND THEM: In small sandy patches within the reef in shallow water.

OBSERVATIONS: Somewhat approachable but able to quickly dive into shelter if danger is close.

COMMON NAME: Halfspotted Goby

SCIENTIFIC NAME: *Asterropteryx semipunctatus*
AVERAGE SIZE: 1 - 2 inches
DESCRIPTION AND DISTINCTIVE FEATURES: Light to dark gray body with numerous blue spots.
DIET: Small crustaceans and invertebrates.
WHERE TO FIND THEM: In shallow, protected, often turbid bays. Rests on the silty bottom associated with dead coral or boat anchorages.
OBSERVATIONS: Allows divers to approach quite closely but takes refuge in a nearby hole.

COMMON NAME: Gorgionian Goby

SCIENTIFIC NAME: *Bryaninops amplus*
AVERAGE SIZE: 1 1/2 - 2 inches
DESCRIPTION AND DISTINCTIVE FEATURES: Almost transparent with seven orange bars on body.
DIET: Zooplankton.
WHERE TO FIND THEM: Found on wire corals or boat mooring lines.
OBSERVATIONS: The female lays an encircling band of eggs on the wire

coral or mooring line, then the male guards the eggs until they hatch.

COMMON NAME: Wire Coral Goby

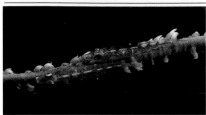

SCIENTIFIC NAME: *Bryaninops yongei*
AVERAGE SIZE: 1 inch
DESCRIPTION AND DISTINCTIVE FEATURES:
Almost transparent body with faint yellow
bars. Distinct red ring around eye.
DIET: Zooplankton.
WHERE TO FIND THEM: On wire coral. These
tiny gobies blend in well, so look closely.
OBSERVATIONS: This species usually occurs in pairs and can be observed darting up
and down the wire coral, rarely leaving it. During reproduction the female goby will
strip part of the coral's tissue, usually near the end, to lay its eggs.

COMMON NAME: Coral Goby

SCIENTIFIC NAME: *Pleurosicya
micheli*
AVERAGE SIZE: 3/4 inch
**DESCRIPTION AND DISTINCTIVE
FEATURES:** Almost transparent
body with internal red stripe.
DIET: Zooplankton.
WHERE TO FIND THEM: Perched
on hard coral below 10 feet,
especially Plate Corals.
OBSERVATIONS: Somewhat

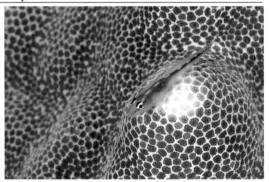

approachable, but able to quickly dart away if danger is close.

COMMON NAME: Golden Goby   E

SCIENTIFIC NAME: *Priolepis aureoviridis*
AVERAGE SIZE: 1½ inches
DESCRIPTION AND DISTINCTIVE FEATURES: Golden-
yellow body with faint darker bars on body.
WHERE TO FIND THEM: Look on ceilings of overhangs, caves and reef crevices below 30 feet. Endemic to Hawaii
OBSERVATIONS: Usually seen in an upside-down
position. Allows divers to approach, but skittish
when an underwater light is used, making it difficult
to photograph.

COMMON NAME: Taylor's or Yellow Cave Goby

SCIENTIFIC NAME: *Trimma taylori*

AVERAGE SIZE: 3/4 inch

DESCRIPTION AND DISTINCTIVE FEATURES: Translucent yellow. Edges of fins have bluish sheen. Dorsal fin has an elongated thread-like filament in males.

WHERE TO FIND THEM: Near the ceiling or side of caves at depths below 30 feet. Uncommon.

OBSERVATIONS: Usually first observed hovering in small, loose schools. Upon divers' approach, the gobies often settle on the cave wall or ceiling.

COMMON NAME: Hawaiian Shrimp Goby **E**

SCIENTIFIC NAME: *Psilogobius mainlandi*

AVERAGE SIZE: 1 1/2 - 2 inches

DESCRIPTION AND DISTINCTIVE FEATURES:
Grayish body with bright blue spots, brownish blotches and lines on mid-section of body.

DIET: Small invertebrates.

WHERE TO FIND THEM: On silty or sandy bottom in shallow protected bays. Endemic to Hawaii.

OBSERVATIONS: Lives symbiotically with a snapping shrimp. The symbiosis benefits both mutually since the goby serves as a guard with its superior vision, warning the shrimp of any potential danger. The shrimp builds and maintains their shared burrow.

COMMON NAME: Fire Dartfish

SCIENTIFIC NAME: *Nemateleotris magnifica*

AVERAGE SIZE: 2 - 3 inches

DESCRIPTION AND DISTINCTIVE FEATURES: Part of dorsal fin extremely elongated. Yellow head with pink markings. White mid-section of body, bright orange rear of body and tail.

DIET: Zooplankton.

WHERE TO FIND THEM: Hovering above the bottom in rubble areas below 550 feet. Rare in Hawaii.

OBSERVATIONS: When approached, Fire Dartfish quickly dive into their burrow for shelter, but the patient diver will soon see them re-emerge. Often occurs in pairs.

COMMON NAME: Spottail Dartfish

SCIENTIFIC NAME: *Ptereleotris heteroptera*

Juvenile

AVERAGE SIZE: 3½ inches

DESCRIPTION AND DISTINCTIVE FEATURES: Greenish-blue body. Large black spot on tail.

DIET: Planktonic crustaceans.

WHERE TO FIND THEM: Known from depths of 20 to 250 feet but are generally found in rubble areas below 60 feet.

Adult

OBSERVATIONS:

When approached too closely Spotted Dartfish quickly dive into their burrow for shelter, but the patient diver will eventually see them re-emerge. Often occurs in pairs.

CHAPTER TEN

Large Bottom Dwellers

Scorpionfishes - Hawkfishes - Lizardfishes
Sandperch - Frogfishes - Flounders- Flying Gurnard

Large Bottom Dwellers

Scorpionfishes - Hawkfishes - Lizardfishes
Sandperch - Frogfishes - Flounders- Flying Gurnard

Family: Scorpionfishes - *Scorpaenidae*

Members of the scorpionfish family are ambush predators, most of them being masters of camouflage. They have no swim-bladder and are usually seen resting on the bottom. Turkeyfish, with their small body and wing-like pectoral fins, are able to hover and swim above the reef while feeding at night. All have more-or-less venomous dorsal spines which can cause severe pain to possibly death in some people due to severe allergic reactions (anaphylactic shock). The good news is that they are very passive animals and would never attack a diver or snorkeler, but due to some species' resemblance to rock, coral, or rubble, you need to be careful where you place your hands.

Photography: All members of the scorpionfish family are a photographer's dream come true. They rarely move and can be successfully photographed with literally all lenses and close up kits on the market, depending on the result you are looking for. Some species are beautiful (Turkeyfish) others bizarre (Devil Scorpionfish) or even "cute" (Leaf Fish), but all provide for the most interesting photographs.

COMMON NAME: Hawaiian Turkeyfish   **E, V**

SCIENTIFIC NAME: *Pterois sphex*

AVERAGE SIZE: 5 - 7 inches
DESCRIPTION AND DISTINCTIVE FEATURES:
Broad reddish-brown bars and narrow white bars along sides of body and fins. Pelvic fins with long spines and short membranes.
DIET: Crustaceans and fishes.
WHERE TO FIND THEM: During the day under ledges and in caverns (check the

ceiling!). At night they emerge onto the open reef. More common than the Hawaiian Lionfish, it is endemic to Hawaii.

OBSERVATIONS: Turkeyfish are shy, but quite approachable and generally don't move unless molested. The dorsal spines are venomous.

COMMON NAME: Hawaiian Lionfish   E, V

SCIENTIFIC NAME: *Dendrochirus barberi*

AVERAGE SIZE: 5 - 6 inches
DESCRIPTION AND DISTINCTIVE FEATURES: Red ring around eyes, two dark bars on greenish-brown and white mottled body. Distinct rows of spots on pectoral fins, membrane covers spines.
DIET: Crustaceans and fishes.
WHERE TO FIND THEM: During the day under ledges and in caverns (check the ceiling!), as well as under rocks on reef flats. At night they emerge onto the open reef. An uncommon species that is endemic to Hawaii.

OBSERVATIONS: Lionfish are shy, but quite approachable and generally don't move unless molested. The dorsal spines are venomous.

COMMON NAME: Decoy Scorpionfish   V

SCIENTIFIC NAME: *Iracundus signifer*

AVERAGE SIZE: 4 - 5 inches
DESCRIPTION AND DISTINCTIVE FEATURES: Mottled red and white body, black spot between second and third dorsal spine.
DIET: Small fishes.
WHERE TO FIND THEM: Rarely seen during the day. On night dives often found in sand and rubble areas deeper than 50 feet.

OBSERVATIONS: Does not move unless molested. Dorsal spines are venomous. When hunting, Decoy Scorpionfish use their dorsal fin as a lure. By moving it from side to side, they create a wavering motion that resembles a small fish.

COMMON NAME: Devil Scorpionfish   V
SCIENTIFIC NAME: *Scorpaenopsis diabolus*

AVERAGE SIZE: 10 - 12 inches
DESCRIPTION AND DISTINCTIVE FEATURES: A humpback-like upper body, an ugly face that resembles a scallop. Brilliant color pattern of orange, yellow and black on inside of pectoral fins.
DIET: Crustaceans and fishes.
WHERE TO FIND THEM: During the day in areas with rubble bottoms.

OBSERVATIONS: When molested, the Devil Scorpionfish will flash the colorful inside of its pectoral fins as a warning. Dorsal spines are venomous.

COMMON NAME: Titan Scorpionfish   E, V
SCIENTIFIC NAME: *Scorpaenopsis cacopsis*

© JAMIE DICKEY

HAWAIIAN NAME: Nohu
AVERAGE SIZE: 15 inches
DESCRIPTION AND DISTINCTIVE FEATURES: Mottled orange body. Fleshy appendages at chin.
DIET: Crustaceans and fishes.
WHERE TO FIND THEM: During the day in rocky areas, often near or underneath ledges and overhangs. Endemic to Hawaii.

OBSERVATIONS: Does not move unless molested. Since this a popular food fish, the impact of spearfishermen makes this species an uncommon find.

COMMON NAME: Shortfinned Scorpionfish   V
SCIENTIFIC NAME: *Scorpaenodes parvipinnis*

AVERAGE SIZE: 3 - 5 inches
DESCRIPTION AND DISTINCTIVE FEATURES: Salmon color with faint dark bars. Sometimes a broad white bar on front of body is visible.
DIET: Small fishes and crustaceans.
WHERE TO FIND THEM: On rubble bottom or on the reef at night, especially near caverns.

OBSERVATIONS: Does not move unless molested. Dorsal spines are venomous.

COMMON NAME: Speckled Scorpionfish   V

SCIENTIFIC NAME: *Sepastapistes coniorta*
AVERAGE SIZE: 1 - 3 inches
DESCRIPTION AND DISTINCTIVE FEATURES:
Numerous dark spots and blotches on
greenish-yellow body. Appears red with
white mottling at night.
DIET: Small crustaceans.
WHERE TO FIND THEM: During the day
these small scorpionfishes hide within the

© GLEN FOWLER

branches of Antler and Cauliflower Coral. This nocturnal fish leaves its shelter at
night to hunt, and may be seen on the open reef on night dives. This scorpionfish is
only found in Hawaii, Wake Island and Line Islands.
OBSERVATIONS: Difficult to observe, due to its habit of hiding within the coral
branches. Does not move unless molested. Dorsal spines are venomous.

COMMON NAME: Leaf Fish   V

SCIENTIFIC NAME: *Taentanotus triacanthus*

AVERAGE SIZE: 2 - 3 inches
**DESCRIPTION AND DISTINCTIVE FEA-
TURES:** Body color may vary from
pink to yellow to white or brown or
even lime green.
DIET: Small fishes and crustaceans
WHERE TO FIND THEM: On the reef in
dead coral areas in or below the surge
zone. Usually close to a small hole
where it can take shelter.

OBSERVATIONS: Does not move unless molested. Dorsal spines are not venomous
enough to harm a diver. Sways from side to side, imitating a piece of seaweed in the
surge.

Family: Hawkfishes - *Cirrhitidae*

With eyes that work independently, hawkfishes are very efficient ambush hunters. As
bottom dwellers that lack a swim bladder, they prey on small fishes and invertebrates. Most species maintain a small territory within which they select 3 - 4 prime
locations to perch on and survey the reef. The male is very territorial and generally
maintains a harem of females. Reproduction occurs by a simultaneous release of eggs
and sperm into the current to be fertilized and carried off into open water.

LARGE BOTTOM DWELLERS

Photography: As bottom dwellers, hawkfishes are quite tolerant in regards to a photographer's approach. Housed camera systems make photographing these fish easy. Trying to place a framer around the animal, however, may be pushing your luck. Perhaps, taking the framer off and just using the wand to measure distance, combined with a lot of patience, may lead to success.

COMMON NAME: Redbarred Hawkfish

SCIENTIFIC NAME: *Cirrhitops fasciatus*

HAWAIIAN NAME: Piliko'a
AVERAGE SIZE: 4 - 5 inches
DESCRIPTION AND DISTINCTIVE FEATURES: Five broad red bars on whitish body. Black spot above pectoral fin. Dark blotch at base of tail. Freckled face . Emerald green eyes.
DIET: Crustaceans and small fishes.
WHERE TO FIND THEM: Most often seen in shallow water perched on a rock, but does occur down to 100 feet.
OBSERVATIONS: Usually quite approachable.

COMMON NAME: Longnose Hawkfish

SCIENTIFIC NAME: *Oxycirrhites typus*
AVERAGE SIZE: 3 - 5 inches
DESCRIPTION AND DISTINCTIVE FEATURES: Stunning crimson crosshatch pattern on white body. Long snout.
DIET: Small planktonic crustaceans.
WHERE TO FIND THEM: On current swept deep water drop-offs. In Hawaii, usually associated with black coral trees and rarely seen above 100 feet.

OBSERVATIONS: Once found, this hawkfish is usually easy to approach.

COMMON NAME: Arc-eye Hawkfish

SCIENTIFIC NAME: *Paracirrhites arcatus*
HAWAIIAN NAME: Piliko'a
AVERAGE SIZE: 4 - 5 inches
DESCRIPTION AND DISTINCTIVE FEATURES: Tri-colored U-shaped arc next to eyes. Color may vary from cream color to dark brown and reddish. Sometimes a broad white stripe is visible on side of body.
DIET: Crustaceans and fishes.

WHERE TO FIND THEM: Inhabits practically all coral reefs in bays, lagoons, and seaward reefs at depths ranging from 5 to 100 feet. Usually seen perched on lobe coral head.

OBSERVATIONS: Allows divers to get very close. If it swims off, it will find another coral head nearby to perch itself on.

COMMON NAME: Blacksided or Freckled Hawkfish

SCIENTIFIC NAME: *Paracirrhites forsteri*
HAWAIIAN NAME: Hilu pilikoʻa
AVERAGE SIZE: 6 - 7 inches
DESCRIPTION AND DISTINCTIVE FEATURES:
Light to dark brown head and front of body covered with red freckles. Broad black stripe on side of body.

Juvenile

Adult

DIET: Small fishes and crustaceans.
WHERE TO FIND THEM: Inhabits practically all coral reefs in bays and seaward areas at depths ranging from 5 to 100 feet. Usually seen perched on Lobe Coral Head.

OBSERVATIONS: Allows divers to get very close. If it swims off it will find another coral head nearby to perch itself on.

COMMON NAME: Stocky Hawkfish

SCIENTIFIC NAME: *Cirrhitus pinnulatus*
HAWAIIAN NAME: Poʻopaʻa
AVERAGE SIZE: 9 - 11 inches
DESCRIPTION AND DISTINCTIVE FEATURES: Mottled body with yellow lines on face and red spots on body.
DIET: Fishes, crabs and other crustaceans.
WHERE TO FIND THEM: Between 10 and 50 feet perched on rocks and coral. Most often seen in the surge zone.

OBSERVATIONS: Often confused with the scorpionfish, due to similar behavior, size and color pattern. This species is the largest hawkfish in Hawaii.

Family: Lizardfish - *Synodontidae* and Sandperch - *Pinguipedidae*

Although not directly related, these two families have many similarities. Sharing the same environment (sand and rubble), these bottom dwellers lack swim bladders and rest on their pelvic fins, surveying the reef. Both have a similar appearance, although lizardfishes look more "reptile-like". As ambush predators they patiently wait for prey to come within striking distance.

Photography: Both fish families are easily photographed with a variety of lenses, depending on their size. At night, when lizardfishes are even more docile, it's possible to carefully approach them with the wand of the close-up kit.

COMMON NAME: Redspotted Sandperch
SCIENTIFIC NAME: *Parapercis schauinslandi*

AVERAGE SIZE: 3 - 4 inches
DESCRIPTION AND DISTINCTIVE FEATURES: White body with two rows of red square spots on side of body.
DIET: Small crabs, shrimps, and large zooplankton.
WHERE TO FIND THEM: In depths below 50 feet, perched on rocks in sand and rubble areas.
OBSERVATIONS: The Redspotted Sandperch is the only shallow-water member of its family in Hawaii. They usually live in colonies of 2 to 6 fish, with one male tending several females. This species is quite uncommon in Hawaii, except for Leeward Oahu and the south Kona Coast.

COMMON NAME: Slender Lizardfish
SCIENTIFIC NAME: *Saurida gracilis*

HAWAIIAN NAME: 'Ulae
AVERAGE SIZE: 8 - 9 inches
DESCRIPTION AND DISTINCTIVE FEATURES: Silvery-gray body mottled with black and white, distinct blotches on rear body. Drab-colored mouth full of bristle-like teeth.
DIET: Small fishes and crustaceans.
WHERE TO FIND THEM: On sandy or silty bottom in protected murky bays and harbors.
OBSERVATIONS: This species is not as commonly observed due to its less attractive habitat.

COMMON NAME: Orangemouth Lizardfish

SCIENTIFIC NAME: *Saurida flamma*

HAWAIIAN NAME: 'Ulae
AVERAGE SIZE: 10 - 12 inches
DESCRIPTION AND DISTINCTIVE FEATURES: Silvery-gray body mottled with bottled with golden brown, and 3 dark blotches on rear body. Bright red mouth, full of bristle-like teeth.
DIET: Small fishes and crustaceans.
WHERE TO FIND THEM: Commonly seen at various depths sitting on sand and rubble areas or live coral.
OBSERVATIONS: Like other lizardfishes, this species is easily approached by divers.

COMMON NAME: Variegated Lizardfish

SCIENTIFIC NAME: *Synodus variegatus*

HAWAIIAN NAME: 'Ulae
AVERAGE SIZE: 8 - 9 inches
DESCRIPTION AND DISTINCTIVE FEATURES: Silvery-gray body mottled with red. Dark blotches on side of body. Mouth has large conical teeth.
DIET: Small fishes and crustaceans.
WHERE TO FIND THEM: Commonly seen at various depths on rocky or rubbly bottoms.
OBSERVATIONS: Easily approached by divers and usually found in pairs.

COMMON NAME: Capricorn Lizardfish

SCIENTIFIC NAME: *Synodus capricornis*

HAWAIIAN NAME: 'Ulae
AVERAGE SIZE: 7 inches
DESCRIPTION AND DISTINCTIVE FEATURES: A row of seven reddish spots along side of body. Reddish bars on lower half of body.
DIET: Small fishes and crustaceans.
WHERE TO FIND THEM: On reefs usually below 60 feet. Only found in Hawaii, Easter Island and Pitcairn.
OBSERVATIONS: Easily approached by divers, but often confused with the Variegated Lizardfish.

LARGE BOTTOM DWELLERS

105

Family: Frogfishes or Anglerfishes – *Antennariidae*

Frogfishes are ambush hunters that normally remain stationary and "fish" for their prey, hence their other common name "anglerfish". The first spine of their dorsal fin is modified as a fishing pole (illicium) with a small piece of flesh (resembling a small shrimp) as bait. The fishing pole is wavered causing the bait to move, and is used to lure the frogfish's prey. As soon as an unsuspecting fish nears, the anglerfish opens its gigantic mouth, creating a vacuum-like suction and swallows the prey with lightning speed. The frogfish can engulf prey that are longer than itself. In case the prey was able to bite off the angler's bait (esca) it simply grows a new one. Frogfishes don't move much, but if necessary can "walk" or "hop" along the bottom or swim in mid-water with a remarkable propulsion system. They swallow huge amounts of water, which is then pushed through narrow gill openings resulting in propulsion. Eggs are released as a gelatinous mass into the current.

COMMON NAME: Commerson's or Giant Frogfish

SCIENTIFIC NAME: *Antennarius commersoni*

AVERAGE SIZE: 7 - 10 inches

DESCRIPTION AND DISTINCTIVE FEATURES: This frogfish can be found in almost any color, with a great variety of algae growing on it, or without any growth. Juveniles look like small blobs of sponge

DIET: Fish and crustaceans

WHERE TO FIND THEM: On the coral reef, resembling a piece of coral, rock or sponge. Look for the eye.

OBSERVATIONS: These frogfishes are one of the most overlooked fishes on the reef, due to their excellent camouflaging abilities. Body color

varies from bright yellow to red, orange, light to dark brown, green and black. They do not have scales, but coarse skin that resembles a sponge. This skin is unique in the ability to collect and grow algae on it. In addition, the frogfish can further camouflage itself by actually growing appendages that resemble hydroids and algae. Periodically the frogfish sheds all growth, probably when it moves to a new territory, and needs to adjust to the new environment. This frogfish rarely moves unless molested.

COMMON NAME: Sargassum Frogfish

SCIENTIFIC NAME: *Histrio histrio*
AVERAGE SIZE: 4 inches
DESCRIPTION AND DISTINCTIVE FEATURES:
Body color brownish-yellow, same color
as Sargassum seaweed. White spots over
entire body. Numerous fleshy
appendages on body.
DIET: Small fishes of the open ocean,
including juveniles.
WHERE TO FIND THEM: In the Atlantic, the
origin of this pelagic frogfish, it is usually
found in sargassum weed, a free-floating
algae that drifts in open water. Since sargassum weed does not exist in Hawaii,
Sargassum Frogfish are often spotted in

When discovering this Sargassum Frogfish in a drifting fish
net we were faced with a bit of a dilemma. By removing
the net from the ocean you take away the frogfish's living
environment and home, by leaving it in the sea it would
continue to present a hazard for other, larger marine life,
as well as boat propellers. We decided to cut it down to a
fraction of its size, and leave the frogfish with a small floating raft.

drifting pieces of fishing net or other debris. It may be found drifting at the surface
near reefs or offshore in the open sea. This is the only frogfish which is not a bottom dweller.
OBSERVATIONS: Does not move unless molested.

Family: Flounders - *Bothidae*

When young, flounders look like "normal" fish larvae, with one eye on each side of
the head. As they mature, the fish's body begins to flatten out and one eye migrates
to the other side. As adults, they are masters of camouflage that are able to perfect-
ly blend into a sandy environment or rubble zone. In addition, they often cover
themselves with sand, leaving only their eyes exposed.

COMMON NAME: Peacock Flounder

SCIENTIFIC NAME: *Bothus mancus*
HAWAIIAN NAME: Paki'i
AVERAGE SIZE: 12 - 15 inches
**DESCRIPTION AND DISTINCTIVE FEA-
TURES:** Blue spots and circles on
grayish, flattened body. Eyes widely
separated laterally on the head.
DIET: Small fishes, crabs and shrimp.
WHERE TO FIND THEM: On flat rocks
or boulders at depths below the

Occasionally Peacock Flounders may be seen swimming over
the reef. At this time they are much easier to spot. They are able
to move surprisingly far and fast.

surge zone. Can also be seen in rubble habitats.
OBSERVATIONS: Often overlooked because of its camouflaging abilities. Color patterns may vary when the fish attempts to match changing terrain. Particularly
noticeable when the flounder swims from a sandy area over a coral reef.

COMMON NAME: Panther or Leopard Flounder

SCIENTIFIC NAME: *Bothus pantherinus*

HAWAIIAN NAME: Paki'i

AVERAGE SIZE: 8 - 10 inches

DESCRIPTION AND DISTINCTIVE FEATURES: Yellow spots circled with blue speckles on grayish-brown mottled body. Pectoral fin of males very long. Eyes not widely separated.

DIET: Small fishes, crabs and shrimp.

This male Leopard Flounder was in the process of courting a female when photographed. Its long pectoral fin spines are raised and visible. (Since the fin appears to be on top of the fish, it's often mistaken as the dorsal fin, but because of the flounder's flattened position, visible top fin is actually the pectoral fin)

WHERE TO FIND THEM: On sandy, sometimes silty patches near the reef.

OBSERVATIONS: Commonly overlooked because of the ability to blend into its sandy environment.

Family: Flying Gurnard - *Dactylopteridae*

Flying Gurnards are related to the Scorpionfish family but do not posses venomous spines. Juveniles are often observed drifting at the surface. At night they become attracted to lights and are often found within the beam of dive boat lights, when preparing for a night dive. As they mature they settle down and become bottom dwellers.

COMMON NAME: Flying Gurnard

©KEOKI STENDER

SCIENTIFIC NAME: *Dactyloptena orientalis*

HAWAIIAN NAME: Loloa'u

AVERAGE SIZE: 10 inches

DESCRIPTION AND DISTINCTIVE FEATURES: Dark spots on light body. Enormously large pectoral fins.

DIET: Crabs and mollusks.

WHERE TO FIND THEM: In sand, rubble and silt environments, often within protected bays or harbors at shallow depths.

OBSERVATIONS: The Flying Gurnard is often seen crawling along the bottom. The gigantic wing-like pectoral fins are spread when threatened, to appear larger to potential predators.

CHAPTER ELEVEN

Silvery and Streamlined

Jacks - Barracudas - Flagtail - Mullet
- Chubs - Snappers - Milkfish

Silvery and Streamlined

Jacks - Barracudas - Flagtail - Mullet
- Chubs - Snappers - Milkfish

Family: Jacks - *Carangidae*

These silvery, strong swimming predators live in open water along outer reef dropoffs. They can be observed visiting the reef when hunting (often at dawn and dusk) or at cleaning stations. The larger species are highly-prized gamefishes.

COMMON NAME: Rainbow Runner

SCIENTIFIC NAME: *Elagatis bipinnulata*
HAWAIIAN NAME: Kamanu
AVERAGE SIZE: 2 feet
DESCRIPTION AND DISTINCTIVE FEATURES:
Streamlined silver body with two blue stripes and yellow tail.
DIET: Small fishes and planktonic crustaceans.
WHERE TO FIND THEM: In blue water along steep walls, occasionally cruising the reef.

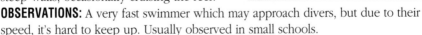

OBSERVATIONS: A very fast swimmer which may approach divers, but due to their speed, it's hard to keep up. Usually observed in small schools.

COMMON NAME: Bluefin Trevally

SCIENTIFIC NAME: *Caranx melampygus*

HAWAIIAN NAME: ʻŌmilu
AVERAGE SIZE: 2 feet
DESCRIPTION AND DISTINCTIVE FEATURES:
Silver body with iridescent yellow and blue mottling and blue fins and tail.
DIET: Small fishes and octopus.
WHERE TO FIND THEM: From shoreline areas to deep water along steep walls, cruising

the reef in search of prey.

OBSERVATIONS: A very strong swimmer which often approaches divers, but wary in areas frequented by spearfishermen. Frequently observed hunting in small groups of three to five trevally and a few blue goatfish. One of the most common jacks on the reef.

COMMON NAME: Bigeye Jack or Trevally

SCIENTIFIC NAME: *Caranx sexfasciatus*

HAWAIIAN NAME: Ulua
AVERAGE SIZE: 25 - 30 inches
DESCRIPTION AND DISTINCTIVE FEATURES: Silver body with white tip on dorsal fin, large eyes.
DIET: Small fishes and crustaceans.
WHERE TO FIND THEM: This night feeder can be seen in dense schools in blue water off steep walls, or singularly cruising the reef at night.

OBSERVATIONS: A very strong swimmer which may allow divers to get close when schooling above the reef.

COMMON NAME: Barred Jack

SCIENTIFIC NAME: *Carangoides ferdau*

HAWAIIAN NAME: Ulua
AVERAGE SIZE: 18 inches
DESCRIPTION AND DISTINCTIVE FEATURES: Silver-greenish body with seven gray bars.
DIET: Crustaceans living at the sea bottom.
WHERE TO FIND THEM: They occasionally cruise into shallow waters of protected murky bays and reefs.

OBSERVATIONS: Often occur in small schools.

COMMON NAME: Black Trevally

SCIENTIFIC NAME: *Caranx lugubrious*
HAWAIIAN NAME: Ulua
AVERAGE SIZE: 30 inches
**DESCRIPTION AND DISTINCTIVE
FEATURES:** Dull-gray body with
dull olive green head. The row
of enlarged scales at rear of body
(scutes) are black and distinctive.
DIET: Fishes.

WHERE TO FIND THEM: Usually seen in deeper water (below 80 feet) near dropoffs
and outer reefs.

OBSERVATIONS: These jacks feed on smaller predatory fishes. Usually not timid when
approached by divers. Sometimes seen in small groups, but more often singularly.
Rare in Hawaiian waters.

Family: Barracudas - *Sphyraenidae*

COMMON NAME: Great Barracuda

SCIENTIFIC NAME: *Sphyraena barracuda*
HAWAIIAN NAME: Kākū
AVERAGE SIZE: 3 - 4 feet
DESCRIPTION AND DISTINCTIVE FEATURES:
Silvery body, protruding lower jaw with
visible teeth. Sometimes has black spots
on lower body. Two black spots on tail.
DIET: Small fishes.

WHERE TO FIND THEM: Usually seen in shallow water above or near the reef.

OBSERVATIONS: In Hawaii most often seen solitary. Their practice of opening and
closing their mouth to aid in respiration gives them a vicious look and a bad reputa-
tion. They also have the intimidating, but harmless habit of approaching divers or
snorkelers and following them around the reef for a while. They tend to move away
if pursued.

COMMON NAME: Heller's Barracuda

SCIENTIFIC NAME: *Sphyraena helleri*
HAWAIIAN NAME: Kawele'ā
AVERAGE SIZE: 2 feet
DESCRIPTION AND DISTINCTIVE FEATURES:
Silver body with two brassy stripes on side
of body.
DIET: Small fishes.

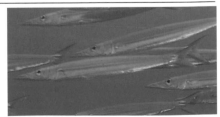

WHERE TO FIND THEM: Near or above the reef.
OBSERVATIONS: Usually seen hovering in large schools.

Family: Flagtail - *Kuhliidae*

This family is not well represented in Hawaii, with the only existing species being endemic.

COMMON NAME: Hawaiian Flagtail　　　　E

SCIENTIFIC NAME: *Kuhlia sandvicensis*
HAWAIIAN NAME: Āholehole
AVERAGE SIZE: 8 inches
DESCRIPTION AND DISTINCTIVE FEATURES:
Silver body with large eyes, dark trailing edge on tail.
DIET: Zooplankton, polychaete worms, insects, algae.
WHERE TO FIND THEM: In very shallow water near shore. Young also occur in brackish water and tide pools. Endemic to Hawaii.
OBSERVATIONS: This night time feeder can be seen forming dense schools during the day. Commonly found in dark caverns along the shoreline or harbor breakwaters.

Family: Mullet - *Mugilidae*

Contrary to trevallies and other silvery fishes, mullets are herbivores. They represented an important food source for ancient Hawaiians.

COMMON NAME: Sharpnose Mullet

SCIENTIFIC NAME: *Neomyxus leuciscus*

HAWAIIAN NAME:
Uouoa
AVERAGE SIZE:
10 inches
DESCRIPTION AND DISTINCTIVE FEATURES:
Silver body with small yellow spot at base of pectoral fin.
DIET: Algae.

WHERE TO FIND THEM: In very shallow water near the shore.
OBSERVATIONS: Usually seen in small schools over sandy, rubbly or rocky bottoms.

Family: Sea Chub - *Kyphosidae*

The Rudderfish is the most common of the sea chubs found in Hawaii. Their natural environment is the shallow surge zone where they school and eat filamentous algae. This fish also has been observed in large schools where humans feed fishes regularly.

COMMON NAME: Rudderfish

SCIENTIFIC NAME: *Kyphosus bigibbus*

HAWAIIAN NAME: Nenue
AVERAGE SIZE: 16 - 20 inches
DESCRIPTION AND DISTINCTIVE FEATURES: Drab silvery-gray body. When excited flashes pattern of oval light spots.
DIET: Filamentous algae.
WHERE TO FIND THEM: In the shallow surge zone to 15 feet.

OBSERVATIONS: Often occurs in schools. Naturally not too approachable, but in areas where fed by snorkel boats, these fish become very bold and approach divers without hesitation. Rudderfish are commonly observed feeding on the algae off an anchored or moored boat.

COMMON NAME: Lowfin Chub

SCIENTIFIC NAME: *Kyphosus vaigiensis*
HAWAIIAN NAME: Nenue
AVERAGE SIZE: 20 - 24 inches
DESCRIPTION AND DISTINCTIVE FEATURES:
Silvery-gray body with rusty stripes and facial markings.
DIET: Filamentous algae.
WHERE TO FIND THEM: In the shallow surge zone to 15 feet.

OBSERVATIONS: Can be observed singularly or in schools. Easily approached by divers and snorkelers. Less common and usually confused with the Rudderfish.

Family: Snappers - *Lutjanidae*
and Emperors - *Lethrinidae*

In Hawaiian waters thirteen different snapper species exist, but most are deepwater species. Divers and snorkelers seldom see more than three or four. Two of the most common species were introduced from French Polynesia in the 1950's as a food source. Commercially the import was a failure, but the species have thrived. Unfortunately it is suspected that the ecological effect has been a negative one for some native species. Emperors, are very closely related to snappers.

COMMON NAME: Bluestripe Snapper

SCIENTIFIC NAME: *Lutjanus kasmira*

HAWAIIAN NAME: Ta'ape
AVERAGE SIZE: 8 - 10 inches
DESCRIPTION AND DISTINCTIVE FEATURES:
Yellow body with four bright blue stripes.
DIET: Crustaceans and small fishes
WHERE TO FIND THEM: Can be seen singularly feeding at night and resting in schools during the day. A very common fish on almost all Hawaiian reefs at any depth.
OBSERVATIONS: This species was introduced as a food source from the Marquesas Islands in 1958. This is a very aggressive fish which, when hand-fed by snorkelers and divers, tends to "take over" the reef. Juveniles can sometimes be seen at depths below 60 feet seeking shelter in small coral islands in sandy areas.

COMMON NAME: Blacktail Snapper

SCIENTIFIC NAME: *Lutjanus fulvus*

HAWAIIAN NAME: To'au
AVERAGE SIZE: 8 - 10 inches
DESCRIPTION AND DISTINCTIVE FEATURES:
Yellow pelvic, dorsal and anal fins. Brassy body and black dorsal fin and tail.
DIET: Crustaceans and small fishes.
WHERE TO FIND THEM: Most common in murky bays and harbors adjacent to reefs.
OBSERVATIONS: This species was introduced as a food source from Moorea in 1958. Not as aggressive or common as the Bluestripe Snapper, and generally found alone. A nocturnal feeder, but can be observed during the day.

COMMON NAME: Smalltooth Snapper

SCIENTIFIC NAME: *Aphareus furca*
HAWAIIAN NAME: Wahanui
AVERAGE SIZE: 12 - 15 inches
DESCRIPTION AND DISTINCTIVE FEATURES: Silver to metallic brown body with yel-

low iris and yellow markings on tail, anal fin and base of pectoral fin.

DIET: Small fishes.

WHERE TO FIND THEM: Cruises high above the reef from 15 to 75 feet.

OBSERVATION: This free ranging predator often allows divers to approach quite closely.

COMMON NAME: Bigeye Emperor or Mu Fish

SCIENTIFIC NAME: *Monotaxis grandoculis*
HAWAIIAN NAME: Mu
AVERAGE SIZE: 12 - 20 inches
DESCRIPTION AND DISTINCTIVE FEATURES: Silvery body with four more or less visible broad bars on upper body.

DIET: Crustaceans and mollusks.

Juvenile

WHERE TO FIND THEM: Hovering above the reef in a resting stage during the day,

Adult

often in loose schools. May be seen at night actively hunting.

OBSERVATION: Upon close observation you will notice the Emperor fish has very human-like teeth. Wary of divers, slowly moving away to maintain a safe distance when pursued.

Family: Milkfish - *Chanidae*

This species is the only one of its family. In ancient Hawaii it was kept in saltwater ponds as a food source.

COMMON NAME: Milkfish

SCIENTIFIC NAME: *Chanos chanos*
HAWAIIAN NAME: Awa
AVERAGE SIZE: 3 feet
DESCRIPTION AND DISTINCTIVE FEATURES: Silver body with distinct, deeply forked tail.
DIET: Floating seaweed, phytoplankton, and algal scums.

WHERE TO FIND THEM: Occurs in a variety of habitats, but is most often observed in the water column above the reef. Frequents areas exposed to current.

OBSERVATION: These large, harmless plankton feeders are often mistaken for sharks by novice divers due to their size and similar shape. Milkfish may allow divers to get close.

CHAPTER TWELVE

Eels

Moray eels - Snake eels - Conger eel - Cusk eel

Eels

Moray eels - Snake eels - Conger eel - Cusk eel

Family: Moray eels - *Muraenidae*
Snake eels - *Ophichthidae*
Conger eel - *Congridae*
Cusk eel - *Ophidiidae*

Eels are elongated fishes with a snake-like body. They have adapted to live in crevices and holes, rarely displaying their entire body in the open. In Hawaii they are quite abundant and represented by many species. Eels tend to be territorial, but do not live in only one hole or location for a lifetime. Due to their habit of constantly opening and closing their mouths, moray eels are often perceived as aggressive. However, this behavior is simply a function of their breathing process. For the most part they are very docile and shy unless provoked or enticed. Certain species of moray eels, such as the Viper, Undulated and Whitemouth, may become aggressive when provoked or fed by divers. Some eels, including the Conger Eel, have crushing plates which are used for eating small crustaceans.

Photography: Since eels generally stay in their hole during the day, many of them are quite willing to model for you, at least for facial shots. Some of the bolder species such as the Yellowmargin and Whitemouth Moray, along with the Conger Eel, may even allow you to place a framer on them. Generally, the more unusual species are timid and more difficult to photograph. By far the most challenging are the shy garden eels, which disappear into their burrow as soon as a diver nears. If you are a videographer, leave your camera in front of an eel's burrow, back off at least 20 feet, and sure enough, the garden eels will reappear and perform for your video. As a still photographer this process is a little more challenging.

COMMON NAME: Yellowmargin Moray

SCIENTIFIC NAME: *Gymnothorax flavimarginatus*
HAWAIIAN NAME: Puhi paka
AVERAGE SIZE: 4 feet
DESCRIPTION AND DISTINCTIVE FEATURES: Light brown body mottled with dark brown. Yellow line along dorsal fin.
DIET: Small fishes, crustaceans, and octopus.

EELS

WHERE TO FIND THEM: At all depths, usually partially hidden in crevices of the reef.

OBSERVATIONS: A common, bold species which has been known to frequent the same areas for up to 30 years.

COMMON NAME: Giant Moray

SCIENTIFIC NAME: *Gymnothorax javanicus*

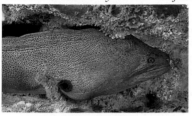

HAWAIIAN NAME: Puhi

AVERAGE SIZE: 6 feet

DESCRIPTION AND DISTINCTIVE FEATURES:
Light brown body with dark squarish spots on head and lower half of body, dark blotches on upper half of body. Note distinctive black spot at gill opening.

DIET: Fishes, crustaceans, and octopus.

WHERE TO FIND THEM: In crevices of the reef at shallow depths. This species is rare in Hawaii.

OBSERVATIONS: Due to its size, this moray is able to inflict serious injuries, when provoked, but normally quite docile.

COMMON NAME: Whitemouth Moray

SCIENTIFIC NAME: *Gymnothorax meleagris*

HAWAIIAN NAME: Puhiʻoniʻō

AVERAGE SIZE: 2 - 3¹/₂ feet

DESCRIPTION AND DISTINCTIVE FEATURES:
White spots all over head and body, inside of mouth is white.

DIET: Small fishes, crustaceans, and octopus.

WHERE TO FIND THEM: At all depths within the recreational dive limit. Look in holes and crevices on the reef and along ledges. If you look out into the distance you may even see one all the way out, moving across the reef.

OBSERVATIONS: This eel is one of the most commonly seen and also one of the boldest. Easily approached.

COMMON NAME: Viper Moray

SCIENTIFIC NAME: *Enchelynassa canina*

HAWAIIAN NAME: Puhi kauila

AVERAGE SIZE: 3¹/₂ - 4 feet

DESCRIPTION AND DISTINCTIVE FEATURES:
Brown body. Very distinctive narrow, hooked jaw with very long teeth.

DIET: Small fishes, crustaceans, and octopus.

WHERE TO FIND THEM: Within crevices of the

EELS

reef at various depths.

OBSERVATIONS: In spite of its vicious appearance, the Viper eel is normally quite docile toward a diver's approach. However, in areas where eels have been fed by man, this species has been known to become very aggressive and should be avoided.

COMMON NAME: Stout Moray

SCIENTIFIC NAME: *Gymnothorax eurostus*

White Phase

HAWAIIAN NAME: Puhi
AVERAGE SIZE: 1 - 2 feet
DESCRIPTION AND DISTINCTIVE FEATURES:
Light body with brown spots. The amount of spots ranges from a few to almost covering the entire body. The light version is often mistaken as a Whitemouth Moray, but lacks the white mouth.

DIET: Small fishes and crustaceans.

Brown Phase

WHERE TO FIND THEM: On the reef at various depths, often hidden in its "puka" (hole in the reef).

OBSERVATIONS: A common species that often remains hidden, with only the head visible. Often overlooked due to its smaller size and drab coloration.

COMMON NAME: Yellowhead or Banded Moray

SCIENTIFIC NAME: *Gymnothorax rueppelliae*
HAWAIIAN NAME: Puhi ʻou
AVERAGE SIZE: 2 - 3 feet
DESCRIPTION AND DISTINCTIVE FEATURES: Top of head mustard yellow. Rest of body features broad dark bands.
DIET: Small fishes, crustaceans, and octopus.
WHERE TO FIND THEM: In bays and seaward reefs at night.

OBSERVATIONS: A nocturnal species that is seldom observed during the day.

EELS

COMMON NAME: Undulated Moray

SCIENTIFIC NAME: *Gymnothorax undulatus*

HAWAIIAN NAME: Puhi laumilo
AVERAGE SIZE: 3 feet
DESCRIPTION AND DISTINCTIVE FEATURES:
Top of head sometimes greenish, other times brown. Similar to Yellowhead Moray, but instead of bars, body features a marbled pattern.
DIET: Small fishes, crustaceans, and octopus.
WHERE TO FIND THEM: In holes and under large rocks at any depth. Most commonly seen at night hunting out in the open.
OBSERVATIONS: A nocturnal species that is seldom observed during daylight hours. It may swim toward divers' lights during night dives, and should be given a wide berth.

COMMON NAME: Slendertail Moray

SCIENTIFIC NAME: *Gymnothorax gracilicaudus*

HAWAIIAN NAME: Puhi
AVERAGE SIZE: 9 inches
DESCRIPTION AND DISTINCTIVE FEATURES:
Body light with irregular brown bars on body and irregular markings on face.
DIET: Small fishes and crustaceans.
WHERE TO FIND THEM: In crevices of the reef usually at night.
OBSERVATIONS: Due to its smaller size this uncommon moray is often overlooked.

COMMON NAME: Barred or Ringed Moray

SCIENTIFIC NAME: *Echidna polyzona*
HAWAIIAN NAME: Puhi
AVERAGE SIZE: 20 inches
DESCRIPTION AND DISTINCTIVE FEATURES: Dark bars on whitish to cream colored background. First bar covers the eye entirely. With age these dark bars become obscure until the pattern becomes a blotchy or mottled lighter brown.
DIET: Mostly small crustaceans.

© RAY MOCK

WHERE TO FIND THEM: An unusual species at scuba depths, the Barred Moray is usually seen on shallow reefs near shore.
OBSERVATIONS: A very shy and attractive species that feeds during the day or night.

EELS

COMMON NAME: Snowflake Moray

SCIENTIFIC NAME: *Echidna nebulosa*
HAWAIIAN NAME: Puhi kapa
AVERAGE SIZE: 2 feet
DESCRIPTION AND DISTINCTIVE FEATURES: White snout with yellow nostrils. Whitish body with black blotches centered around yellow markings.

DIET: Crabs and other crustaceans.
WHERE TO FIND THEM: From tidepools to depths around 90 feet, these less common morays can be seen using rocks for cover and protection. More abundant in areas of dead coral.
OBSERVATIONS: This moray does not possess sharp teeth. It is usually shy and timid when approached resting, but can be aggressive when feeding in the open.

COMMON NAME: Dragon Moray

SCIENTIFIC NAME: *Enchelycore pardalis*

HAWAIIAN NAME: Puhi kauila
AVERAGE SIZE: 2 - 3 feet
DESCRIPTION AND DISTINCTIVE FEATURES:
Fleshy, horn-like nasal appendages. Curved jaws with sharp teeth. Striking color pattern includes spots and blotches ranging from white to brown, red and black.
DIET: Crustaceans and small fishes.
WHERE TO FIND THEM: Generally on reefs among Finger Coral, in depths ranging from 30 - 100 feet and possibly deeper. Most often only the head is visible. Rare in Hawaii.
OBSERVATIONS: A very shy species which will retreat if a diver approaches too quickly.

COMMON NAME: Zebra Moray

SCIENTIFIC NAME: *Gymnomuraena zebra*
HAWAIIAN NAME: Puhi
AVERAGE SIZE: 3 feet
DESCRIPTION AND DISTINCTIVE FEATURES: Brown body encircled by white rings. Teeth are not sharp, but pebble-like and designed to crush prey.
DIET: Crabs and shrimp.
WHERE TO FIND THEM: On the reef at depths below 10 feet.
OBSERVATIONS: This species is uncommon, but

may be observed in the open. Quite shy when sheltering under rocks and coral.

COMMON NAME: Tiger Moray

SCIENTIFIC NAME: *Scuticaria tigrinus*
HAWAIIAN NAME: Puhi
AVERAGE SIZE: 3 feet
DESCRIPTION AND DISTINCTIVE FEATURES: A
cream to flesh colored body covered with
round purplish brown blotches.
DIET: Small fishes and crustaceans.
WHERE TO FIND THEM: In crevices of the reef,
primarily at night.

OBSERVATIONS: A very secretive nocturnal eel that is only occasionally observed.
Often only parts of the body are visible, while the head and tail remain hidden within
the protection of the reef.

COMMON NAME: Pencil or Dwarf Moray

SCIENTIFIC NAME: *Gymnothorax melatremus*

HAWAIIAN NAME: Puhi
AVERAGE SIZE: 8 inches
DESCRIPTION AND DISTINCTIVE FEATURES:
Small size, mustard colored head, sometimes
dark markings on body, but that part is rarely
seen. Note iridescent blue iris.
DIET: Small crustaceans.
WHERE TO FIND THEM: In cracks and crevices
on the reef at various depths.

OBSERVATIONS: Often mistaken for baby eels,
but a full-sized adult of this species is no longer than 10 inches. A very shy, but common species that is seldom seen out in the open.

COMMON NAME: Spotted or Magnificent Snake Eel

SCIENTIFIC NAME: *Myrichthys magnificus*
HAWAIIAN NAME: Puhi lāʻau
AVERAGE SIZE: 2 - 3 feet
**DESCRIPTION AND DISTINCTIVE FEA-
TURES:** Slender white body covered with
brown oval spots. Pointed snout with
small eyes.
DIET: Small crustaceans and small fishes.
WHERE TO FIND THEM: In areas of dead
coral, rubble, and mixed sand and rock.
OBSERVATIONS: Often seen probing in

and out of reef crevices in a snake-like manner. Responds indifferently to the
approach of divers.

COMMON NAME: Crocodile Snake Eel

SCIENTIFIC NAME: *Brachysomophis crocodilinus*
HAWAIIAN NAME: Puhi
AVERAGE SIZE: 2½ - 3 feet
DESCRIPTION AND DISTINCTIVE FEATURES: Head white, white with red markings, or bright red. Body red or pale with dark brown spots on upper half. Visible teeth. Eyes high and forward.

DIET: Small fishes and crustaceans.
WHERE TO FIND THEM: In the sand at various depths within the recreational dive limit.
OBSERVATIONS: This odd-looking snake eel lives under the sand and only leaves its head exposed. As an ambush hunter it relies on its camouflage to capture prey. Only found in certain areas on a regular basis.

COMMON NAME: Conger Eel

SCIENTIFIC NAME: *Conger cinereus*

HAWAIIAN NAME: Puhi ūhā
AVERAGE SIZE: 4 feet
DESCRIPTION AND DISTINCTIVE FEATURES: Thick lips, gray head and body. At night dark bars along body become visible. Has no sharp teeth but crushing plates. Pectoral fins present.
DIET: Fishes, crustaceans, and octopus.
WHERE TO FIND THEM: During the day under ledges and in large crevices at any depth. After dark this nocturnal species can be seen out in the open searching for food.
OBSERVATIONS: Generally responds with curiosity towards divers. Appears to have very poor eyesight.

COMMON NAME: Cusk Eel

SCIENTIFIC NAME: *Brotula multibarbata*
HAWAIIAN NAME: Palahoana
AVERAGE SIZE: 1½ feet
DESCRIPTION AND DISTINCTIVE FEATURES:
Brownish body with several pairs of white barbels on snout and chin.
DIET: Small fishes and invertebrates.
WHERE TO FIND THEM: On the reef, generally at night when they emerge to feed.
OBSERVATIONS: This very secretive eel is rarely observed during the day. At night divers sometimes catch a glimpse of it, but as soon as you shine your light at them they return to a crevice, thus making it very difficult to observe or photograph.

Sharks
and Rays

Sharks and Rays

Family: Sharks - *Carcharhinidae/Sphyrnidae/ Rhincodontidae/Hemigaleidae*

Sharks are some of the most fascinating and graceful creatures in the sea. At the top of the ocean's food chain, sharks have evolved from prehistoric times and are essential in maintaining the balance of our underwater ecosystem. Unfortunately, sharks are being slaughtered and killed at a rate of over 100 million annually. Due to this senseless shark killing and overfishing (mostly to please the demand in the Orient, where shark fins are used for soup), the worldwide population is dwindling quickly. As you can see, humans are a much bigger problem for sharks than they are to us. Unlike other large marine animals, such as dolphins and whales, sharks suffer from negative public opinion due to fear and ignorance. The movie "Jaws" forever sealed the public's opinion on sharks. Besides being an unrealistic story, the movie portrayed only one of 375 species of sharks, of which only a handful are even considered dangerous to man. Sharks are very sophisticated hunters that do not normally pursue humans, and when attacks occur they are often caused by confusion--a surfer resembling a sea lion from the shark's point of view; a spearfisherman that won't give up speared fish the shark is after. Most shark species, especially reef sharks, are quite shy and present no danger to divers. In fact, most divers consider themselves lucky when a shark is encountered.

Sharks, unlike most other fishes, have a skeleton made of cartilage, rather than bone. This cartilage allows them the flexibility to spin their head back to their tail in an instant. A good reason not to pull their tail. Sharks possess gill slits instead of the typical gill plates of bony fishes. They lack a swim bladder and gain their buoyancy through the skillful use of their fins and oily livers. Many species need to keep swimming continuously in order to "breathe", which requires them to constantly pass water over their gills. Sharks also have extremely sharp senses. They can smell and hear prey in distress from great distances and hone in on it. At close range they pick up electrical fields emitted by all living organisms. Reproduction is quite advanced with pups being born fully developed, avoiding the larval stage other fishes must pass through. But unlike fishes who reach maturity quickly and produce thousands or millions of eggs, sharks take many years to reach maturity and then only reproduce a few pups a year.

Photography: Most sharks are fast swimmers, and seldom allow divers to approach closely. Ideally a 15mm or 20mm wide angle lens is used, but a 28mm-85mm (or similar) zoom lens is another excellent option. Stationary Whitetip Reef Sharks are commonly found in caverns and under overhangs and can be quite cooperative when photographed. Free-swimming sharks are often encountered at depth, with very little light and contrast available. When using autofocus, try to focus on the eye or another high contrast part of the shark.

COMMON NAME: Gray Reef Shark

SCIENTIFIC NAME: *Carcharhinus amblyrhynchos*

HAWAIIAN NAME: Manō
AVERAGE SIZE: 6 feet
DESCRIPTION AND DISTINCTIVE FEATURES:
Black band on tail.
Gray body.
DIET: Fishes, crustaceans, and cephalopods.
WHERE TO FIND THEM:

Patrolling reefs in clear water, often along dropoffs and deeper depths.
OBSERVATIONS: Not commonly seen in Hawaii. Tends to be curious, but should not be pursued when displaying threatening behavior (arched back, pectoral fins lowered).

COMMON NAME: Whitetip Reef Shark

SCIENTIFIC NAME: *Triaenodon obesus*

HAWAIIAN NAME:
Manō lalakea
AVERAGE SIZE:
2 - 5 feet
DESCRIPTION AND DISTINCTIVE FEATURES:
White marking on dorsal fin and tail.
DIET: Fishes, crustaceans, and cephalopods.
WHERE TO FIND THEM:
This is the shark most commonly encountered in Hawaii. Usually found resting on sand under ledges or in caverns.
OBSERVATIONS: A very docile species, that allows close approach, but will swim away, when disturbed.

COMMON NAME: Scalloped Hammerhead Shark

SCIENTIFIC NAME: *Sphyrna lewini*

HAWAIIAN NAME: Manō kihikihi
AVERAGE SIZE: 8 - 10 feet
DESCRIPTION AND DISTINCTIVE FEATURES:
Distinctly shaped hammer-like head.
DIET: Fishes including other sharks, as well as octopus and squid and perhaps turtles.
WHERE TO FIND THEM: This is a coastal species and is usually observed by chance encounter when they approach the reef to visit a cleaning station, mate, or pup. Can be a problem for spearfishermen.
OBSERVATIONS: Sometimes responds with curiosity towards divers but usually wary and maintains its distance. Enters murky bays and harbors during summer months.

COMMON NAME: Oceanic Whitetip Shark

SCIENTIFIC NAME: *Carcharhinus longimanus*

AVERAGE SIZE: 5 - 6 feet
DESCRIPTION AND DISTINCTIVE FEATURES: Long rounded pectoral and dorsal fins with white markings.
DIET: Pelagic squid and fishes such as tuna and Mahimahi.
WHERE TO FIND THEM:
This is a pelagic species that occurs in the ocean's

surface layers and is encountered by fishermen a few miles offshore. On very rare occasions these sharks visit the reef and may be seen by divers in shallow water.
OBSERVATIONS: This is a very bold shark and should not be aggravated. Best to stay out of the water when close by.

COMMON NAME: Whale Shark
SCIENTIFIC NAME: *Rhinocodon typus*

AVERAGE SIZE: 25 - 40 feet
DESCRIPTION AND DISTINCTIVE FEATURES: Gigantic size, white spots all over black body.
DIET: Zooplankton, pelagic squid, small fishes.
WHERE TO FIND THEM: Reaching up to forty feet in length this pelagic species is known to cruise near the reef from time to time. It is also just as likely to be spotted several miles offshore. They travel the currents in search of plankton to feed upon. January seems to produce the most frequent encounters, but it's a possibility at any time of the year.
OBSERVATIONS: This is the largest fish in the world. As a plankton feeder, it is harmless and makes for a thrilling experience for snorkelers or divers.

Family: Rays - *Myliobatidae/Mobulidae*

Related to sharks, rays are cartilaginous fishes with greatly enlarged pectoral fins. Since these fishes do not possess a swim bladder, their oversized fins are used for swimming and hovering. Rays are simply awe-inspiring when "flying" over the reef, like a mysterious, prehistoric bird. None of the rays in Hawaii are aggressive and can be observed up close whenever encountered.

Photography: Manta rays often allow divers to get as close as they dare. In that case, a 15mm or 20mm wide angle lens is your ideal choice. For shy rays, or smaller species, such as the eagle ray, a 35mm or 50mm lens is a good option. A 28mm-85mm zoom lens can be ideal.

COMMON NAME: Spotted Eagle Ray

SCIENTIFIC NAME: *Aetobatis narinari*

HAWAIIAN NAME: Hīhīmanu
AVERAGE SIZE: 4 - 6 1/2 feet
DESCRIPTION AND DISTINCTIVE FEATURES: White spots on black back.
DIET: Hard-shelled invertebrates.
WHERE TO FIND THEM: Cruising the reef, dropoffs or sand flats.
OBSERVATIONS: In sandy areas this ray may be observed digging for food. They may be encountered singularly, in small groups, or on rare occasions in large schools. In most cases does not allow divers to get close. Do not try to ride. Eagle rays have several barbs at the base of the tail for protection.

COMMON NAME: Manta Ray

SCIENTIFIC NAME: *Manta birostris*

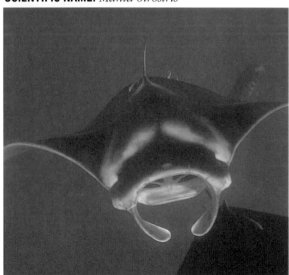

HAWAIIAN NAME: Hahalua
AVERAGE SIZE: 8 - 15 feet
DESCRIPTION AND DISTINCTIVE FEATURES: Horn like protrusions. Black spots on white belly.
DIET: Zooplankton and small fishes.
WHERE TO FIND THEM: These are the mantas that made "Manta Ray Village" on the Kona Coast famous. Most nights up to 9 mantas gather outside Keauhou Bay where, for years, the Kona Surf Resort has lit the shallow water with spotlights.

The light attracts the plankton, which in turn attracts the mantas.
During the day look toward the blue water when diving a dropoff; you may see one cruise by. Also occasionally seen when visiting a cleaning station on the reef.
OBSERVATIONS: When feeding, these mantas ignore divers and often pass within a couple of inches. Occasionally they are observed leaping into the air. Do not try to grab or ride.

Glossary

Ambush hunters
Species that lay motionless waiting to attack by surprise.

Benthic
Plants or animals that live on the sea bottom.

Barbel
A tentacle-like sensory organ located on the chin of fishes such as the goatfish.

Caudal peduncle
Region of the body where it is attached to the tail fin.

Cirri
Eyelash-like appendages on the head of blennies and hawkfishes.

Gills
The respiratory organ of fishes (and other aquatic animals) that breathe oxygen dissolved in water.

Invertebrates
Animals without a backbone, such as lobsters, nudibranchs, worms.

Lateral line
Horizontal row of pressure-sensitive structures on a fish's flank.

Nocturnal
Primarily active at night.

Pelagic
Fishes that live free-swimming in the open ocean, rather than near the reef or sea bottom.

Plankton
Tiny pelagic plants (phtyoplankton) and animals (zooplankton), sometimes in the larval stage, that drift with the currents.

Polychaete
Segmented worms that may be free living or residing in a tube.

Swim or Gas bladder
An internal organ in fishes that is used to control buoyancy.

About The Authors

With a degree in education, Casey Mahaney and his partner Astrid Witte have a combined twenty years of experience in the dive and snorkel industry. After issuing over a thousand scuba certifications and introducing tens of thousands of reef watching enthusiasts to the intricacies of the reef, they are well aware of the marine life information divers and snorkelers seek. As enthusiastic underwater naturalists and photographers, they have made it their goal to provide literature on marine life identification and behavior -- specializing in a style that is convenient, easy to understand, as well as entertaining.

Their photography and dozens of articles have been published in magazines worldwide, including Aqua Geographica, Skin Diver, Ocean Realm, Sportdiving, Aquanaut, Tauchen and many others. They are also the authors of *Reefwatchers Hawaii, Reefwatchers Guam & Micronesia, Hawaiian Reef Fish - The Identification Book*, and *The Essential Guide to Live-Aboard Dive Travel*. Many of their photographs are on display in art galleries throughout the Hawaiian Islands.

Their company, **Blue Kirio Travel**, offers scuba adventure tours to remote and exciting Pacific destinations, all personally escorted by Casey and Astrid. For up-to-date schedules and information, contact the authors at:

BLUE KIRIO TRAVEL
74-5602 Alapa Street # 764
Kailua-Kona, HI 96740
(800) 863 2524
e-mail: caseym@interpac.net
http://www.bluekirio.com

Index

Large Bottom Dwellers

Large Ovals and Discs

Oddshaped Swimmers

Reddish, Bigeyes

Sharks and Rays

Silvery and Streamlined

Swims with Dorsal Fin

References

Church, J. *Essential Guide to Nikonos Systems.* New York: Aqua Quest Publications, 1994.

Fielding, A., and E. Robinson. *An Underwater Guide to Hawaii.* Honolulu: University of Hawaii Press, 1987.

Hoover, J.P. *Hawaii's Fishes.* Honolulu: Mutual Publishing.

Lieske, E., R. Myers. *Coral Reef Fishes.* Princeton: Princeton University Press.

Mahaney, C. *Hawaiian Reef Fish, The Identification Book.* Kailua-Kona: Blue Kirio Publishing, 1993.

Myers, R.F. *Micronesian Reef Fishes.* Guam: Coral Graphics.

Randall, J.E. *Shore Fishes of Hawaii.* Vida: Natural World Press, 1996.

Russo, R. *Hawaiian Reefs.* San Leandro: Wavecrest Publications, 1994.

Wilson, R. and J.Q. Wilson. *Watching Fishes.* Houston: Gulf Publishing Company, 1992.

Witte, A. and C. Mahaney. *Reefwatchers Hawaii, Fish & Critter I.D.* Kailua-Kona: Blue Kirio Publishing, 1996.

Wu, N. *How to Photograph Underwater.* Mechanicsburg: Stackpole Books, 1994.